Praise for
The Gift of Rest

"What a wonderful book! Reading it helped me to recapture the wonder and excitement I experienced when I first became a Sabbath observer some thirty years ago. Senator Joe Lieberman and David Klinghoffer provide insights that can enrich anyone's life, not just weekly but daily."

—Michael Medved, nationally syndicated talk radio host author of *The 10 Big Lies About America*

"What a wonderful service Joe Lieberman has rendered his frazzled fellow Americans by reminding them of God's gift of the Sabbath. *The Gift of Rest* has certainly convicted this too-busy Baptist to mend his ways and once again embrace a weekly 'day of rest.'"

—Richard Land, President of the Southern Baptist Convention's Ethics & Religious Liberty Commission

"*The Gift of Rest* is a charming, beautifully written inspirational gem, as well as a fascinating insider's look at how spirituality and faith intersect at the highest echelons of political power."

—Jonathan Kellerman, bestselling novelist

"This charming, personal, and informative book by the popular Senator Joe Lieberman 'is my love song to the Shabbat,' the Jewish Sabbath, and what it can mean for non-Jews as well. This discovery and rediscovery of the Shabbat offers an intimate glimpse into the mind and heart of a decent and thoughtful person, written in non-technical prose, and which cannot fail to inspire a sensitive reader. Read it and cherish it. It will add a new dimension to your life."

—Rabbi Dr. Norman Lamm,
Chancellor of Yeshiva University
Rosh Hayeshiva (Head) of the Rabbi Isaac Elchanan
Theological Seminary

"Joseph Lieberman does not just acknowledge the Sabbath as a break from the working week. As an observant Jew he relishes and bathes in the spirit of it. While most other faiths do not embrace the formal rituals of Judaism, there is much here that we can admire and that will remind Christians of what we have lost as respect and love for the Sabbath has diminished. This is a book about faith that both informs and transforms the reader."

—Cecil O. Samuelson, President of
Brigham Young University

"What a beautiful book about a beautiful concept—a day of rest as a gift to humanity. Senator Lieberman's account of the Sabbath brought back fond memories of my own past while inspiring me to try to return to the values embodied in the Sabbath."

—Alan Dershowitz,
author of *The Trials of Zion*

THE GIFT *of* REST

Rediscovering the Beauty of the Sabbath

SENATOR JOE LIEBERMAN

with David Klinghoffer

In conjunction with OU Press

OU**PRESS**

HOWARD BOOKS
A DIVISION OF SIMON & SCHUSTER, INC.

New York • Nashville • London • Toronto • Sydney • New Delhi

Howard Books
A Division of Simon & Schuster, Inc.
1230 Avenue of the Americas
New York, NY 10020

First Howard Books hardcover edition August 2011

HOWARD and colophon are trademarks of Simon & Schuster, Inc.

For information about special discounts for bulk purchases, please contact Simon & Schuster Special Sales at 1-866-506-1949 or business@ simonandschuster.com

The Simon & Schuster Speakers Bureau can bring authors to your live event. For more information or to book an event, contact the Simon & Schuster Speakers Bureau at 1-866-248-3049 or visit our website at www .simonspeakers.com.

Manufactured in the United States of America

10   9   8   7   6   5   4   3   2   1

Library of Congress Cataloging-in-Publication Data

Lieberman, Joseph I.
   The gift of rest : rediscovering the beauty of the Sabbath / Joe Lieberman with David Klinghoffer ; in conjunction with Orthodox Union.
      p.   cm.
  1. Lieberman, Joseph I.—Religion. 2. Sabbath. 3. Rest—Religious aspects—Judaism. 4. Work—Religious aspects—Judaism. I. Klinghoffer, David, 1965- II. Union of Orthodox Jewish Congregations of America. III. Title.
   BM685.L5125 2011
   296.4'1—dc22   2010053831

ISBN 978-1-4516-0617-1
ISBN 978-1-4516-0618-8 (ebook)

Unless otherwise indicated, all Scripture quotations are taken from the *Koren Tanakh*. Hebrew names from this Bible translation have been changed to English names for ease of reading. Scripture quotations marked KJV are taken from the King James Version of the Bible. Public domain. Prayer book quotations are taken from the *Koren Siddur*. Chapter 1 quotation is taken from *Genesis Rabba* by Joseph Neusner.

FOR

HADASSAH FREILICH LIEBERMAN

my wife, soulmate, and partner
in accepting, guarding, and enjoying
God's gift of Sabbath Rest
and for
our children and grandchildren
to whom we pass the gift

Said the Holy One Blessed Be He to Moses:
Moses, in my storehouse I have a goodly gift,
and the Sabbath is its name.
—Talmud, *Beitzah* 16a

CONTENTS

AUTHOR'S NOTE

I know some people will wonder why a United States Senator is writing a book about a religious subject like the Sabbath, and others will ask why a Jewish senator is writing a book about the Sabbath for Christians and people of other faiths as well as for Jews. The reason is simple: I love the Sabbath and believe it is a gift from God that I want to share with everyone who reads this book, in the hopes that they will grow to love it as much as I do.

The pioneering Zionist and Hebrew writer Ahad Ha'am famously remarked that, "More than the Jews have kept the Sabbath, the Sabbath has kept the Jews." Certainly in my personal life I have found that to be true. When people ask me: "How can you stop all your work as a senator to observe the Sabbath each week?" I answer: "How could I do all my work as a senator if I did *not* stop to observe the Sabbath each week?"

I am, of course, not a rabbi or trained religious scholar. You may wonder, then, about the sources I drew on in writing this book. I am a religiously observant Jew who has over the years learned from many people who are wiser and more erudite than I. Most of those people are mentioned in the text before you, as are the sources in Scripture and rabbinic law and commentary that shape my Sabbath observance and thought.

When I write about the Sabbath, it is not merely my opinion that I seek to convey but the distillation of a great and ancient tradition. Jewish tradition is a fount of authoritative biblical interpretation and wisdom with origins stretching back to Abraham and Moses, who learned from God Himself. Over the course of more than three thousand years, prophets and sages have transmitted this wisdom from teacher to student, parent to child, later to be recorded in the Talmud, Midrash, and other rabbinic works.

I am deeply grateful to everyone who has helped me with this book, but of course, I take full responsibility for everything in it.

Stamford, Connecticut
April 3, 2011

THE GIFT OF THE SABBATH

I t's Friday night, raining one of those torrential down-pours that we get in Washington, D.C., and I am walking from the Capitol to my home in Georgetown, getting absolutely soaked. A United States Capitol policeman is at my side, as we make our way up Pennsylvania Avenue from the Capitol building toward our distant goal, a four-and-a-half-mile walk. Before leaving my Senate office I changed into sneakers, but now they are full of water.

As we slosh forward, a Capitol police car travels alongside for extra security at a stately pace. But I do not—indeed I cannot—accept a ride in the car.

What accounts for this strange scene? The presence of the two policemen is easily explained. As the Senate's sergeant at arms, who oversees the Capitol police, once said to me, "Senator, if something happens to you on my watch while you're walking home, it will be bad for my career." So that's why the police are with me.

But why am I walking instead of riding on a rainy night? Because it's Friday night, the Sabbath, the day of rest when observant Jews like me do not ride in cars. That would vio-late the letter and spirit of the Sabbath laws as the Bible and

Jewish rabbinical opinions make clear. Normally I get home from my work in time for the start of the Sabbath—*Shabbat* in Hebrew, or *Shabbos* in Yiddish—at sundown on Friday. But on this occasion, important votes on the budget of the United States kept me from doing so. Voting in the Senate is conducted the old fashioned way, by voice, and there are no proxies. You can't vote on behalf of one of your colleagues. If I miss an important vote, it would mean that on that particular issue the people of my home state of Connecticut would lose their representation. They would lose their say in the running of our country, the spending of their tax payments, or the safety and quality of their lives. That is something my religious beliefs tell me I cannot allow, even on the Sabbath, so when there are votes in the Senate after sundown on Friday, I vote and then I walk home.

I've taken this long walk from the Capitol to my home on thirty or forty occasions in my twenty-two-year senatorial career. The police officers who accompany me normally provide not only security but welcome companionship and conversation. Many are devout Christians. The journey takes about an hour and a half, and we've had some wonderful discussions about the Sabbath in particular and faith in general. But not tonight. It's just too wet and miserable to talk much. It is now 10:00 p.m., and my police escort and I take a break and slip under the shelter of a convenience store awning.

At that moment, I must admit, I looked to the heavens from which rain continued to pour and asked, half in humor and half in sincerity, "Dear God. Is this really what you want me to be doing to remember and honor the Sabbath?"

That's not a question I often feel compelled to ask. Observing the Sabbath is a commandment I have embraced, the fourth commandment to be exact, which Moses received from God on Mt. Sinai. Most of the time, it feels less like a commandment and more like a gift from God. It is a gift I received from my parents who, in turn, received it from their parents, who received it from generations of Jews before them in a line of transmission that goes back to Moses.

For me, Sabbath observance is a gift because it is one of the deepest, purest pleasures in my life. It is a day of peace, rest, and sensual pleasure. By *sensual* I don't mean *sexual*—though you might find it interesting to know that one religious "responsibility" given to every married Jew is to make love with their spouse on the Sabbath because this is meant to be a day on which we experience the fullness of life. My wife Hadassah once mentioned this to a couple of women friends who were startled by the revelation.

"Oh," said one, her eyes going wide, "I wish my husband would become more religiously observant."

When I said the Sabbath is sensual, I meant that it engages the senses—sight, sound, taste, smell, and touch—with beautiful settings, soaring melodies, wonderful food and wine, and lots of love. It is a time to reconnect with family and friends—and, of course, with God, the Creator of everything we have time to "sense" on the Sabbath. Sabbath observance is a gift that has anchored, shaped, and inspired my life.

So, you might ask, if it's such a gift and pleasure, why not just get in the car with the policemen and take an easy, eagerly offered ride home? The book you hold in your hands is my answer to your question.

The Sabbath is an old but beautiful idea that, in our frantically harried and meaning-starved culture, cries out to be rediscovered and enjoyed by people of all faiths. It takes the form it does—its laws and customs—because from ancient days, generations of rabbis and sages have been transmitting, refining, and elaborating traditions that define Sabbath observance. These traditions build fences—like not riding in a car—around the Sabbath to protect it as a day of faith and rest. The Sabbath is an organic entity reflecting centuries of thought and experience. It is not an arbitrary contrivance. Some ordinances may have seemed meaningless in the past, but they have been revealed in their full meaningfulness in modern times. I constantly seek the wisdom of Sabbath practices, and I'm rarely disappointed by what I find. If the cost is an occasional inconvenience or discomfort—like getting soaked on the walk home from the Capitol—I consider that a small price to pay for all the Sabbath gives and teaches me.

Hadassah and I sometimes speak of a place beyond time called "Shabbatland." In many ways, the Sabbath is an entirely different place from the one in which we live our weekday lives. It's a place away from clocks and watches, bound only by the natural movements of the sun. Whether I am spending Shabbat in Washington, D.C., or in my hometown of Stamford, Connecticut, entering the Sabbath is like stepping into a different world defined not by geographical boundaries but by faith, tradition, and spirituality.

"On Shabbat," Rabbi Menachem Mendel Schneerson, the rebbe (or chief rabbi) of the Chabad Lubavitch movement, said, "we cease to struggle with the world, not because the task of perfecting it is on hold, but because on Shabbat, the world *is* perfect; we relate to what is perfect and unchanging in it."

In speaking with Christian friends, especially in the Evangelical and Roman Catholic communities, I've felt an appreciation for the gifts of Sabbath observance and a desire to spread them. Some have asked me, "Why do you observe the Sabbath?" and "What do you do on the Sabbath?" I now propose to answer them and you through the prism of the Hebrew Bible which most Christians call the Old Testament and which provides the shared wellsprings from which we draw our faith.

In the Torah, the Bible's first five books, we are given the text of the fourth commandment twice: once in Exodus, when Scripture narrates the revelation of God to the children of Israel at Mt. Sinai, and again three books later in Deuteronomy when Moses repeats the story of the Sinai revelation to the Israelites in the desert forty years later. The wording of the commandment in these two accounts is different.

Exodus emphasizes the role of the Sabbath in commemorating the *creation* of the world and in acknowledging and honoring God as Creator. We are told there to "remember" the Sabbath, to remember particularly that the world has a purposive Creator. We are not here by accident. We got here as a result of God's creation.

The second recording of the commandment to observe the Sabbath is in the context of God's liberation of the Jewish people from Egypt. It is an affirmation that God not only created us but that He continues to *care* about His creation and about human history:

And remember that thou wast a servant in the land of Egypt, and that the Lord, thy God brought thee out from there with a mighty hand and a stretched out arm: therefore the Lord thy God commanded thee to keep the Sabbath day. (Deuteronomy 5:15)

The Exodus led to the revelation at Sinai in which the commandment to remember and guard the Sabbath is given. And with the law came the responsibility each of us has to become God's partners in shaping, improving, and ultimately perfecting human history.

This book is my love song to Shabbat. The best way I can sing this song and really make a case for the day I love is by showing you Shabbatland, by giving you a tour of a typical Sabbath day.

The Sabbath officially begins on Friday evening at sundown and ends on Saturday at nightfall. Like a symphony with its different parts, Shabbat also has its "movements"—distinct phases of the day. I count nine of these, formally beginning on Friday night with *Kabbalat Shabbat*, the Welcoming of the Sabbath Bride, and concluding on Saturday night with the ceremony called *Havdalah*, which means Separation. *Havdalah* is the moment when the conclusion of the Sabbath separates the holiness of the Sabbath from the ordinary weekday that follows.

But in a very real sense, the Sabbath begins during the day on Friday, which we call *Erev Shabbat*, the eve of the Sabbath, a time of intensive practical and, one hopes, spiritual preparation. Shabbat officially concludes at "nightfall" Saturday night (rather than at sundown, which is earlier) when we enter the six days of work that follow the day of rest. As I take you on your guided tour of Shabbatland, we'll start with Sabbath Eve and proceed from there. We'll experience the day together, the faith and feelings and the meanings and practices of a typical Sabbath.

Before we start our tour, I want to offer you a point of clarification and welcome. This book is for both Jews and non-Jews, whatever their personal religious observances may be, because the fourth commandment and its gift of Sabbath rest were given to all people. In fact, as we go along you'll see that the Sabbath provides answers to the most difficult questions people of all faiths have asked themselves for generations: How did I get here? Does anyone care how I behave? What will happen to me after I die?

The prophet Isaiah taught beautifully about a future time when everyone will observe the Sabbath:

> Also the sons of the stranger, that join themselves to
> the Lord, to serve Him, and to love the name of the
> Lord, to be His servants, every one that keeps the
> Sabbath and does not profane it. . . . Even them will
> I bring to My holy mountain, and make them joyful
> in My house of prayer. (Isaiah 56:6–7)

Then in the concluding verses of his book, Isaiah pictures how it will be in that blessed future:

> And it shall come to pass, that every new moon, and
> every Sabbath, shall all flesh come to bow down to
> the ground before Me, says the Lord. (Isaiah 66:23)

The Sabbath is a gift from God to all people. In our time, I believe, it is a gift that is desperately needed.

In this book, we will explore some of the immense and fascinating complexities of traditional Jewish Sabbath observance and thought. Still, the Sabbath is *not* an all or nothing proposition. It offers to enrich your life and give you rest in direct proportion to how much of its spirit and practice you choose to incorporate into your life. But I warn you: a single taste of Sabbath can lead you to want more. As we go along, I will explain the Sabbath as I know it and offer practical advice—"Simple Beginnings"—on some easy ways to adopt aspects of Sabbath observance in your own life. I hope that the more you experience its pleasures, the more you will want to remember, guard, and enjoy God's day.

Now, join me please on a journey to and through the Sabbath day.

Chapter One

SABBATH EVE:

PREPARATIONS, PHYSICAL AND SPIRITUAL

Friday Afternoon

Whether I'm in Stamford or Washington, I try to get home earlier on Friday than any other day of the week so I can participate in preparing for the Sabbath. But I don't always make it as early as I hoped. Sometimes when I walk into the kitchen, my wife, Hadassah, will be on the phone with one of our kids. "Oh, Daddy just walked through the door," she says with a wry glance in my direction. "He said he'd be home at two-thirty. Oh, look, its four already!"

In accordance with Jewish tradition, I always bring flowers home for Hadassah and our Shabbat table on Fridays. A Capitol Hill newspaper once surveyed members of Congress, asking, among other things, "Do you ever buy your wife flowers?"

"Yes," I said.

"How often?"

"Every week," I answered.

"Oh my goodness," said the reporter, "you are so roman-tic!" The resulting article nominated me as one of the most romantic members of Congress.

I like to think of myself as romantic, but flowers on Friday afternoon is as much a gesture of respect and love for Shabbat as it is one of respect and love for my wife. The beauty and smell of the flowers—even the ritual of stopping at the Safe-way in Georgetown or the Stop & Shop in Stamford to pick them up—is part of my preparation for the Sabbath.

Of course Hadassah is well ahead of me in getting ready. The forbidden labors of the Sabbath—thirty-nine categories, all detailed by the rabbinical authorities of long ago—are cre-ative activities that imitate God's creativity in the first six days. They include lighting a fire, and by extension, light-ing an electric light or using a combustion engine like the one that makes your car move. Handling money is forbidden on Shabbat, and we don't go shopping or engage in busi-ness. Cooking is prohibited, so Hadassah prepares the Sabbath meals on Thursday night and/or Friday.

The Sabbath does not just happen spontaneously at sun-down on Friday. In some important ways, it begins as dark-ness falls on the preceding Saturday night and we prepare to return to the six days of work. We leave Shabbat, knowing it is our responsibility to be as creative and purposeful for the next six days as God was in creating the Heaven and Earth. But we also yearn to return to Shabbat to enjoy the gift of rest, just as God enjoyed the seventh day as the culmination of His creation.

By Thursday night Hadassah has decided on a plan of ac-tion for our meals. By Friday afternoon all is ready, and the wonderful smells of food fill the house. The dining room table is set with our best china, embellished by the flowers I have brought.

⚘ MEMORIES OF SHABBAT ⚘

My earliest memories of Shabbat are in my grandmother's house—where we lived until I was eight years old. On Friday morning and afternoon, the house was busy with activity and cooking and cleaning, as if we were preparing for the arrival of a very honored guest.

In 1950, Mom and Dad, along with my sisters Rietta and Ellen and I, moved into our own house on Strawberry Hill Court in Stamford, about two miles north of my grandmother's. The warm, rich Sabbath memories continued there. Of all the blessings I have received in my life, the first was one of the best—maybe the best ever. I was blessed to be born the son of wonderful parents, Henry and Marcia Lieberman. They were loving, supportive, and principled. They taught my sisters and me a lot, and gave us a lot, including the gift of Sabbath rest and observance.

Mom and Dad came from very different religious backgrounds, but together they created a unified, religious home. My mother's family was very observant. My dad's was not. My father's mother, Rebecca, died in New York in the influenza epidemic in 1918 when he was only three, and his father, Jacob, put him into an orphanage for Jewish boys where he stayed until he was ten. When his father remarried and moved to New Haven, he brought my father and his sister, Hannah, to live there with his new wife and her children.

Dad's family was very secular, so he received no religious education and didn't even have a Bar Mitzvah. He graduated from high school in 1933 in the Depression, but though he was intellectually brilliant, he could not go to college. Instead he took a series of jobs that began on an overnight delivery truck for a bakery in Bridgeport and culminated in a factory in Stamford, where at a Purim dance (celebrating the story of Queen Esther) at the Stamford Jewish Center, he met Mom. When they got engaged, two members of her family who owned liquor stores offered to help Dad lease and open his own liquor store. They all agreed that as soon as he was making twenty-five dollars a week, they could get married. That incentive system worked well, and they married in 1940. It was only before their wedding—at the insistence of my mother's family—that Dad took lessons and had his Bar Mitzvah. Although he came to Judaism later in life, his faith was deep and informed. He studied religious texts and commentaries, often in his liquor store between customers, and became quite learned. Later he joined a class in modern conversational Hebrew and became fluent. He loved the Sabbath, but as was the custom for many men at the time, he kept his liquor store open on Friday night and Saturdays because he could not afford to close. For most of my childhood, Dad would try to come home early for dinner on Friday and break for lunch on Saturday, but was otherwise not at home or synagogue on the Sabbath.

Dad was a deductive believer in God, founding his faith in God's existence on the extraordinary sophistication and order of the natural world and on the miraculous continuity and survival of the Jewish people in the human world. Neither, he concluded, could have happened without divine support.

Dad created the intellectual basis for my religious observance, and Mom provided the spiritual depth and traditional ritual-blessed home environment to which my faith attached itself and grew. Together, they built a very spiritual home, with great pleasures and high expectations for my sisters and me. The Friday pre-Shabbat experiences that I first had in my grandmother's house continued and grew in Mom and Dad's house.

I would come home from school on Friday afternoon and immediately inhale the aroma of the chicken soup, meat, or *kugel*—a sweet baked noodle dish—or whatever else was cooking. I would go over to the stove and pick up the lid of the chicken soup pot, smell it, and then take a spoonful. Years later, when Hadassah first saw me tasting from the soup pot on Friday afternoon in my mother's kitchen, she was appalled.

"How can you do that!" she asked in her most mannerly New England tone.

"It's my tradition," I answered, with a big smile as if I was Tevye in *Fiddler on the Roof*. But Hadassah was unconvinced.

Later I learned I had the Code of Jewish Law on my side. It may surprise you that Judaism has such things codified, but one highly authoritative legal commentary, the *Mishnah Berurah*, actually says, "It is meritorious to taste every dish on Erev Shabbos, so as to see that it is prepared well and properly." Little did I realize that I had such esteemed authority to justify my undisciplined Friday afternoon ardor for chicken soup.

The Midrash, a compilation of ancient rabbinic traditions, tells the story of a Roman Emperor, named Antoninus Pius, who had a close friendship with Rabbi Judah HaNasi (the prince), the head of the Jewish community in the land of

Israel at the end of the second century. Rabbi Judah served him a delicious meal when the emperor visited him on Shabbat. On another occasion, Antoninus visited on a weekday. Although the food was as elaborately prepared as before, it did not taste nearly as good. When the emperor mentioned this, Rabbi Judah replied that unfortunately each dish was missing a very special ingredient. The emperor then asked: Why did you leave out the ingredient this time? Were you skimping on costs? Rabbi Judah replied: The missing spice is the Shabbat. Food prepared and eaten in the ambience of the Sabbath has a special, delicious flavor which we cannot duplicate at a weekday meal (*Genesis Rabba* 11:4).

In the opening scene in Marcel Proust's *Remembrance of Things Past*, the narrator tastes a cookie, a madeleine, that he associates with his childhood and that spontaneously fills him with memories and sensations. When it comes to the Sabbath, we taste or smell or see or hear, and immediately we are transported to Shabbatland—as Hadassah and I call it—with all its religious, mystical, and sensual meanings and memories. So when I walk into Hadassah's kitchen today and smell the baking *challah*, the specially braided bread of Shabbat, I am instantly transported to the kitchen of another woman whose influence on me was so crucial that, without it, I might not be a Sabbath observer today.

My maternal grandmother, Minnie, or "Maintza" as she was known in Yiddish, was the religious foundation of our home. I associate her with many things, of course, but preparing for Shabbat is high on that list. We spent the first eight years of my childhood living on the second floor of her house. We called her Baba, a Yiddish word for "Grandma." After we moved into a home of our own, Baba would spend most

Sabbaths with us. She would appear at our door on Friday afternoon, Erev Shabbat, with a towel full of pastries or a pot full of some other food she had made for us. I can almost smell the pastries—the sweet, crescent-shaped *rugelach*—and the wonderful firm, little sugar cookies. She often brought us *challah*, along with delicious chicken soup.

Baba was one of the most patriotic Americans I have ever known. Like countless other immigrants to this country, she had something to compare America to—the place from which she came. There, she and her family were poor and religiously harassed. Here, she found opportunity and acceptance. One of the most miraculous experiences of her life, she once told me, was when her Christian neighbors in our ethnically diverse neighborhood would see her walking to synagogue on Saturday morning and say, "Good Sabbath, Mrs. Manger." At those moments, Baba probably thought she was not in Connecticut, but in heaven.

Years later in 2000, on the first Sabbath after I accepted the Democratic nomination for vice president, Hadassah and I and some of our kids ended up in Lacrosse, Wisconsin. As we walked through the lovely streets from our hotel to the local synagogue on Saturday morning, people came out of their homes to wish us a good Sabbath. I thought of Baba and how right she was to be a grateful and patriotic American.

By the time of her passing away in 1967, at age eighty-six, she had moved into our house full-time. The very last words Baba spoke on the day of her death were about honoring Shabbat by preparing for it. I was in law school at Yale and clearly remember being called that Friday afternoon and told that Baba had suffered a serious stroke and that I should rush back to Stamford. On the last Erev Shabbat of Baba's life, my mother later told me, she and Baba were in the kitchen. Baba, sitting idly at the table, said to my mother, "Masha, give me something to do *l'kavod Shabbos*," which means to honor the Sabbath. My mother gave her some carrots and onions to chop for the soup. She was chopping vegetables *l'kavod Shabbos* when she fell ill for the last time. She died that Friday night, on Shabbos, which tradition says is a special blessing for the righteous.

At that time in my own life, I had fallen away from Sabbath observance. During my first semester as an undergraduate at Yale, I was sincerely worried that I would flunk out. I hadn't yet realized that to get kicked out of Yale for poor grades actually required quite a determined effort. I could have easily taken time off from my school work on Shabbat, but anxiety about my academic performance, combined with peer social pressures not to be different, pulled me away in surprisingly short order, and I stopped observing the Sabbath. Ironically, I still put on *tefillin*, the little black leather boxes filled with sacred scrolls that observant Jewish men wear on their arms and head for morning prayer, and said my prayers each morning. Why did I do one and not the other? Maybe, I must admit, it was because putting on *tefillin* was private and personal, and Shabbat was more public and interrupted the weekend social flow of college life.

During college, I continued to observe the Jewish dietary laws, but by the time I reached law school, I also began straying in my eating. When I look back at this time, I am amused and a bit embarrassed by the strange distinctions I made. I would eat non-kosher chicken or beef, but never with milk because the mixing of meat and milk products is an additional prohibition in the Torah. I continued to refrain from ham, bacon, or shellfish, except on one memorable occasion. Someone convinced me to try Lobster Newburgh. After all, I reasoned, the lobster was removed from its familiar shell and cloaked in a rich sauce, therefore making it unrecognizable to both me and God. I took one mouthful of the shellfish, chewed it, swallowed it, and immediately proceeded to the men's room where I puked up everything in my stomach. I suspect my stomach upset had more to do with theology and psychology than with gastronomy or gastroenterology.

My Baba's death in 1967 marked the beginning of my return to Jewish observance. There was a synagogue right across the street from where I had lived for more than a year in New Haven, Connecticut but I had never gone there. The Shabbat after Baba passed away, I remember saying, "I really want to go to *shul*"—*shul* is the Yiddish term for synagogue.

Was it because of my grandmother's last words, which so hauntingly conveyed her love of preparing for the arrival of Shabbat? Perhaps indirectly. But uppermost in my mind was the worry that Baba was my link with the Judaism of my ancestors, the Judaism of history. If I let go of the link in the chain, it would be broken and lost to me and my children after me. And so I slowly began my return to regular synagogue attendance and Sabbath and religious observance.

When I think of Erev Shabbat, I think also of Baba's husband, my grandfather. His name was Joseph Manger. I am named for him and therefore never knew him because we Jews of European ancestry name for deceased relatives or friends. He died when my mother was just a child and he was only forty-two; his death, too, was strangely linked to Sabbath observance.

My grandfather started in the soda business in Stamford,

and like many Jewish immigrants at that time he decided that supporting his family ruled out giving up that day of work on Saturday. He had been a very religiously observant man in Europe, and in 1922, he finally reached a time in America when he felt he could afford to stop working on Shabbat. It happened that year that the two-day Jewish festival of Shavuot—which like the Christian Pentecost, occurs fifty days after the beginning of Passover—began on Sunday evening. So to prepare for the festival, my grandfather went to the market on Friday and bought a live fish that the family planned to cook on Sunday and eat on Shavuot. In the meantime, over Shabbat, the fish lived in a bathtub full of water in their home. This is how things were done at that time.

On Friday night, my grandfather went to *shul* for prayers, excited that he was beginning the first Sabbath he would fully observe in his new country.

"I will never break Shabbos again," he told his wife and children, including my mother, who was then seven years old.

He was so proud, so pleased. When Saturday morning came, he went to the synagogue to pray and hear the Torah read. Then he returned home for the festive lunch meal during which he complained to his wife, my Baba, of a pain in his arm. It must have been no ordinary pain because she told him he should visit the local physician, Dr. Nemoitin, at his office—which was in his home—between the afternoon and evening prayers of the Sabbath. My mother always remembered Baba and her four siblings walking her father to the corner that day as he returned to *shul* for the afternoon service. As he walked, he carried his infant son, my Uncle Ben. When they got to the corner, he handed my uncle to Baba, crossed the street, and smiled broadly as he and the family happily wished each other a "Good Shabbos."

They never saw him alive again.

Following the afternoon service, on his way to the doctor's office, he crossed the street and was struck by a bicycle and thrown onto some trolley tracks, badly hitting his head. Maybe that was the cause of his death, or maybe the pain in his arm was a symptom of an impending heart attack. In any case, he ended that Shabbat, the last of his life and the first he was ever to observe fully in America, in the hospital where he died later that night.

He had said he would never break Shabbat again and, of course, he never did. In my family, the story of Joseph Manger's death always concludes with the ironic—and perhaps mystical— observation that on Sunday morning, after my grandfather's life on earth ended, the fish he had purchased before Shabbat was still very much alive, swimming in the family bathtub.

So both of my mother's parents left me with a legacy, from their lives and deaths, of preparing for the Sabbath and enjoying it.

❧ SACRED PREPARATIONS AND DELIGHTS ☙

Since we are forbidden to cook on the Sabbath, we need to get our food ready before the sun goes down. This practice creates a feeling of anticipation. If you were expecting an honored guest to visit your home, what would you do? You would spend hours before his or her arrival in intensive preparation. You would vacuum. You would dust. You would mop. You would cook or purchase fine food and some good wine. All would be in order well in advance of your guest's arrival.

Even more significant are the preparations for the Sabbath, since we are preparing metaphorically and spiritually for the arrival of the most eminent guest in the world—the King of Kings. On Shabbat we feel as if we are receiving God into our homes with gratitude and love. The intensity of our experience is proportional to, among other things, the intensity of our preparation. We prepare ourselves inwardly not just by praying or meditating but also by doing physical things. In general, this is the Torah's approach: the path to changing the inner you—your feelings and attitudes—is taking positive physical action.

There is a long tradition that speaks of this with regard to the Sabbath. The prophet Isaiah said,

> If thou restrain thy foot because of the Sabbath, from pursuing thy business on My holy day; and call the Sabbath a delight, the holy day of the Lord honorable; and shalt honor it, not doing thy own ways, nor pursuing thy own business, nor speaking of vain matter, then shalt thou delight thyself in the Lord. (Isaiah 58:13–14)

The sages of old tell us that the words "delight" and "honor" refer to twin aspects of Sabbath observance. We *delight* in Shabbat on the day itself. But we *honor* it by preparing our homes and ourselves beforehand.

The physical aspect of Sabbath preparations has become increasingly important in our contemporary world where so many of us do so little physical labor. Today, jobs that leave our hands unsoiled by manual labor are increasingly common. We live in the information age, so working with information—a nonphysical entity—leaves a lot of us without the experience of real, old-fashioned labor for most of the week. Now more people work with ideas rather than with physical objects. Certainly that describes my work as a senator. Probably more than most people, I'm exempted from physical tasks. But not when it comes to preparing for the Sabbath.

When I stop at the supermarket for flowers, I often also buy a few last minute pre-Shabbat necessities or treats for the family, maybe some cookies or chocolate. When I get home, I try to help prepare the house for our Shabbat guests. I might get out my shears and trim the bushes by the side of our house or weed the garden or sweep the garage and driveway. Since we are not permitted to boil water on Shabbat, I always boil the water for instant coffee or tea, then put it in an electric urn to keep it hot over the Sabbath. I turn on the lights we want to stay on during Shabbat and turn off those we don't, including the one in the refrigerator that we don't want to go on each time we open the door. The Code of Jewish Law emphasizes that even if a person has household help, he should engage in manual preparations for Shabbat himself. The rabbis of the Talmud, who lived more than fifteen hundred years ago either in Israel or Babylonia, were the ultimate example of those who work with ideas rather than with their hands. But when it was time to get ready for Shabbat, they rolled up their sleeves. The Talmud lingers appreciatively over details of what these long-ago sages did to honor Shabbat. One put on a special black smock to show he was ready to get dirty. Another salted the fish. Others twined wicks for the lamps, lit the lamps, minced the beets, split the wood, lit the fire, or carried bundles into and out of his home. In a curious detail, the sage Rav Safra is said to have sought out the task of singeing the head of the animal that was to be eaten for the Shabbat meal. This was done to remove any hair or feathers. It was presumably a nasty-smelling task.

Hadassah and I try to eat in a health-conscious way, but we make small allowances for some errant but tasty consumption on Shabbat. This is in the spirit of "delighting" in the Sabbath. The Code of Jewish Law says that "depending on one's means, he should prepare a considerable quantity of meat, wine and delicacies."

Acquiring special foods for Shabbat is an activity that starts early in the week. In fact, the whole week is occupied, to one degree or another, with the anticipation of the Sabbath. The Sabbath day is separate and unique, but never far from our hearts and minds on the other six days.

The Jewish liturgy instructs us to say a different psalm at the end of each morning's prayer service. It is the psalm that the Levites sang in the Temple on that day. "Today is the first day of the Sabbath week," we begin on Sunday. "Today is the second day," we say on Monday, and so on. We literally count the days to Shabbat, the way an eager child counts the days to a favorite holiday or to a birthday. One rabbi of old, Shammai, had the custom of seeking out some delicious food each day of the week and setting it aside for the Sabbath. This was because he interpreted the verse from the fourth commandment, "Remember the Sabbath day to keep it holy," as meaning to do something every day of the week in preparation for Shabbat. If on a later day, he found an even tastier morsel, he would eat what he had already put aside and substitute the superior food for Shabbat. He repeated this procedure daily until he reached the Sabbath. Thus, each day of the week, he sought to eat in honor of Shabbat.

There are many other nonedible ways to "remember the Sabbath" throughout the week. One custom I have is putting reading material that is not urgent but that I definitely want to read into a specially marked folder. Shabbat is a time for rejoicing and resting but also for contemplating—reading and thinking. Reading is not one of the thirty-nine forbidden labors, but obviously if I were going over the details of a piece of legislation that I meant to propose for passage in the Senate during the next week, for example, that would take me out of the Sabbath mood. But in my "Shabbat Reading" folder I gather items of less pressing or workaday interest—articles and memos that my staff has forwarded to me or that I discover on issues I find important, intriguing, or stimulating. If there is time I also enjoy reading a good book on Shabbat. This, too, takes preparation, buying, and setting things aside for Shabbat.

If all this sounds pedestrian or even shallow, there is another side to Sabbath preparation that is intended to ready us spiritually for the special day to come. The rabbis teach that Friday afternoon, *Erev Shabbat,* is a time for introspection, thinking about what kind of week we have had. Did I do right by my family, friends, and co-workers? Did I do right by God? It is an important time for self-examination and even repentance. The *Mishnah Berurah*'s language on this is strong. Since we are about to greet the King, "it is not fitting to receive Him vested in the tattered rags of the illness of sinfulness."

Each Friday afternoon, time allowing, I try to take a second shower of the day or—if there is enough time—a bath. I put on fresh clothes and give myself some time for spiritual preparation for the Sabbath. One of my favorite pre-Shabbat traditions is reading King Solomon's Song of Songs, that passionate poem of love between God and the children of Israel.

But the hard truth is that there is often frenzy in the air as the clock mounts steadily toward the time when Sabbath candles are lit, shortly before sunset, signaling the start of the Sabbath. I once saw a bumper sticker on a car that read, "RELAX! THE SABBATH IS COMING." Hah! That's a fine sentiment for the other six days, but in reality, relaxing is the last thing there's time to do when you are preparing for Shabbat.

Getting ready in the last couple of hours before sundown on Friday can be stressful, especially during the short days of winter, and if you have little children it can be a test of the peacefulness we all want to enjoy in our homes. Hadassah and I are past the stage of tending to our children before Shabbat—our kids are now all grown with children of their own—even so, we are not always the picture of relaxation as the Sabbath approaches.

One tradition Hadassah and I have is to phone each of our children and grandchildren wherever they happen to be on Erev Shabbat, unless of course they are with us, to wish them a good Shabbat and to give Sabbath blessings to them. Some of our grandchildren like us to sing with them the Shabbat songs they have learned in school like "*Shabbat Shalom* (Peaceful Sabbath), *hey! Shabbat Shalom, hey!*"

❧ SUNSET BEGINNINGS ❧

Many people have asked, "Why does the Sabbath day begin with the coming of night?" In our familiar weekday world, some view the day beginning at midnight. Others think of it as beginning at sunrise—a new day, a new sun. In Colonial times, many Americans followed the Jewish way of thinking on this. According to the historian Benson Bobrick, the Christian Sabbath was then regarded as beginning at sundown Saturday night. Some early American Christians also concluded their Sabbath as Jews customarily conclude theirs—at the appearance of three stars on Sunday evening.

So why does the Sabbath begin at sunset?

The first reason is that the Hebrew calendar is luni-solar, that is, it is a lunar calendar that is coordinated with the solar calendar, so (unlike the Muslim lunar calendar) the seasons of each holiday remain matched to the solar calendar. Passover always comes out in the spring and Rosh Hashanah—the New Year—is always in the fall. In lunar calendars the day starts with the appearance of the moon at night. But there is a deeper more spiritual reason as well: night is perceived by many as a time of trial, worry, and dread. Even King Solomon, for all his wealth and might, was troubled by nighttime. The biblical Song of Songs speaks of the terror of the night. Of Solomon's own bed, we read, "Sixty valiant men are round about it, of the mighty men of Israel. All girt with swords and expert in war: every man has his sword upon his thigh because of the fear by night" (3:7–8). By contrast, the rising of the sun is a time of relief and rejoicing: "It is a good thing to give thanks to the Lord . . . to relate Thy steadfast love in the morning, and Thy faithfulness every night" (Psalm 92:2–3).

A beautiful insight recorded by the rabbis in the Midrash, which draws lessons from and offers additional narrative to that in the Bible, teaches that Psalm 92 was composed by the first man, Adam. According to the Midrash, Adam was created by God in the Garden of Eden, then sinned and was sentenced to be expelled from the Garden all in one day—on Friday, the sixth day of creation. When the sun went down that evening, he and Eve were filled with terror. According to this teaching, he had never seen darkness before. He assumed that the light was going out of the world because of his sin. He feared it was the end of creation, the end of the world. And it was all his fault. Imagine how terrified, how full of guilt and remorse, he was all that night.

But the sun came up the next morning! Imagine his relief, his joy. The sun for him, as for us, bore a message of hope and redemption. "Thus," Chief Rabbi Sir Jonathan Sacks of the United Kingdom has written, "Shabbat is as close as we come to Paradise regained." The rabbis say that Adam sang this song, Psalm 92, as a hymn to God, thanking Him for the hope God had given man that light would always follow darkness.

God gave us the Sabbath as a gift, and He meant for us to enjoy it. We begin the holy day with darkness so that we can more fully appreciate the light of the Sabbath day when it dawns.

❧ The Significance of Seven ❧

Because the Sabbath is the seventh day, it signals to us the coming of freedom, redemption, and salvation. As my friend and teacher Rabbi Menachem Genack has pointed out to me, the Torah is full of sevens—cycles of seven days, seven weeks, and seven years. Unlike the natural movement of the sun that defines each day and the natural movement of the moon that defines each month, there is no reason in nature that a week should be seven days. Clearly, God meant something important by decreeing that the six days of labor followed by a seventh day of rest would make a week. In the Bible, seven is a code word, or symbol. It signals the state of completion or the arrival of perfection. Thus the arrival of Shabbat is meant to complete and perfect the life we have been leading all week long.

Seven weeks from the beginning of Passover, the Torah commands that we observe the festival of Shavuot, which commemorates the receiving of the Ten Commandments at Mt. Sinai. Our march to freedom was completed when we accepted the divine discipline to lead good lives. Spiritual freedom completes political and cultural freedom. Similarly, a sabbatical year was observed every seven years. A Jubilee year was celebrated at the conclusion of seven times seven years. These celebrations of seven each bring with them various forms of liberation—cessation from work, the freeing of slaves, the forgiving of debts. The verse recorded on our Liberty Bell in Philadelphia, "Proclaim liberty throughout all the land unto all the inhabitants thereof," is from Leviticus (25:10) and describes the freeing of slaves on the occasion of the Jubilee year.

❦ THE FREEDOM OF LAW ❧

God offers us freedom on the Sabbath, the seventh day. It may seem paradoxical that freedom is achieved by adhering to laws, but that is another great lesson of the Bible. The liberation of the Israelites from Egyptian slavery was only the first part of God's reentering human history. Freedom without purpose and law too often leads people to degeneracy or chaos. The Israelites and all of mankind were given their mission and destiny when Moses received the Law from God on Mt. Sinai, including the commandment to remember and guard the Sabbath. Our true freedom as human beings is dependent on our acceptance of the responsibility to serve God by obeying His laws. The laws of the Sabbath, which we will explore in detail in the following chapters, may seem burdensome at first glance, but without them, the gift of rest that comes with the Sabbath would be almost impossible to enjoy. Let me make this point personal: if there were not a divine law commanding me to rest, I would think of many good reasons to go about my normal routine on Friday night and Saturday. That is my nature. I am, for example, addicted to my BlackBerry.

Six days a week, I'm never without this little piece of plastic, chips, and wires that miraculously connects me to the rest of the world and that I hope makes me more efficient, but clearly consumes a lot of my time and attention. If there were no Sabbath law to keep me from sending and receiving email all day as I normally do, do you think I would be able to resist the temptation on the Sabbath? Not a chance. Laws have this way of setting us free. So on Friday as sunset approaches I turn off the television, the BlackBerry, the computer, and the phones as one of the final acts of preparation for Shabbat. It is all about making a separation between the six days of labor and the seventh day of rest, which in itself is a reminder of one of the Bible's greatest lessons: God's law constantly challenges us to make separations, to make choices, to see the difference between right and wrong, good and evil, Sabbath rest and the week of work, light and darkness.

❧ THE SABBATH LIGHT ❧

In our home, the Sabbath officially begins when Hadassah lights the two Sabbath candles, the last creative act until nightfall on Saturday. Why candlelight and not electric lights? Why should our last creative act of Erev Shabbat be the creation of fire? Part of the reason is that fire is the original and true light of Creation. Part is that with the entrance of the "Sabbath Queen"—the Talmud's ancient personification of the Sabbath, in relationship to God as our cosmic King— we are welcoming an older, gentler, and timeless light, the soft, mellow candle, which replaces the modern, sharp, and artificial light of the computer, the television, and the Black-Berry screen.

Every generation has its own pharaoh and its own slave masters, uniquely based on the culture of the time. Our pharaoh may be the electronic devices—computers, televisions, iPhones—that mesmerize us, dominating hour after hour of our lives. Our eyes and faces are glued to one screen or another for much of every day. Even when we think we are at leisure, they invade our attention, holding us in their grip and separating us from our family and friends—sometimes from our faith. Too often they show us an electronic alternative reality full of negativity, trivia, or degradation. From all this, the Sabbath offers to free us for a twenty-four-hour period.

Traditionally, the Sabbath candles are lit by the woman of the home, but they can be lit by a man if no woman is present. Hadassah puts a shawl on her head and says the prescribed blessing, "Blessed are you Lord our God, King of the universe, who commanded us to light the Sabbath lamp." As she lights the candles, she covers her eyes with her hands and thinks first about our children and grandchildren and then about our parents and loved ones who have passed away, sending out prayers for the peace of the Sabbath to them all.

And then, suddenly, the frenzy and stress end. It is Shabbat.

"Shabbat Shalom!" we greet each other and exchange Sabbath hugs and kisses. "Sabbath Peace to you."

Welcome to Shabbatland.

Now we invite you to go with us to our synagogue for the evening service to greet the Sabbath.

❦ SIMPLE BEGINNINGS ❦

⧉ Get your house ready for your own version of Sabbath rest. Before the special day arrives, buy flowers or make sure that the room where you'll enjoy your family meal is tidy and clear of clutter. If you have a dining room, eat there rather than in the kitchen.

⧉ Plan ahead. Whether dinner, lunch, or both, cook and get everything else in order for the meal. Some Christian families make preparation of Sunday lunch or dinner a family activity.

⧉ Sometimes invite extended family and friends to your Sabbath meal; other times let it be an intimate experience just for your spouse and yourself and your children. If you're not married, make dinner for a close friend and enjoy each other's company at home rather than going out to a restaurant.

⧉ Consider adopting a particular favorite dish or two to prepare regularly for your weekly Sabbath. The taste and smell will come to be associated with your special meal.

⧉ During the week before your Sabbath, try to do something "in honor of the Sabbath" even if—*especially* if—it's still six, five, or four days away. For example, buy a food delicacy or a special bottle of wine and put them away to enjoy on the Sabbath.

- Set aside some particularly enjoyable and relaxing Sabbath reading.

- On the eve of your Sabbath, read from the Bible, perhaps the Song of Songs, or other evocative religious texts.

≈ Chapter Two ≈

KABBALAT SHABBAT:

WELCOMING THE SABBATH

———————————

Friday Evening Service

As we move to the synagogue for Friday evening services, I want to share an important life lesson I learned from my Sabbath observance—one I needed to learn before I could accept the gift of rest.

≈ MAINTAINING BOTH CAREER AND FAITH ≈

None of us needs to work every day of the week. A lot of people think they are perpetually indispensable—to their families, to their co-workers, to themselves, maybe even to the world. If I don't go to work, my career will be ruined. If I don't go shopping, my family will starve. If I don't go to the gym, my body will atrophy.

The truth is that we—and the world—will survive just fine if we stop working or shopping and stay home with our families one day a week. Our lives will continue. Our careers will go forward. Our families will flourish. This is true even for members of the U.S. Senate, men and women with a greater tendency to think of ourselves as indispensable than most. The fact is that none of us is essential every minute of the week. I am here to testify that laying your work aside for one day a week is a responsible and ultimately productive choice. This big Sabbath lesson and insight may be as humbling and anxiety-producing for you as it used to be for me, but it is ultimately liberating.

It might seem that desisting from work and other weekday activities on the Sabbath would make it harder to advance your career and would sour your relationships with co-workers, customers, or constituents. I worried about that too. It is true that after I was elected to my first public office as state senator in 1970 and began turning down invitations to political or community events on Friday evenings and Saturdays, people were puzzled, frustrated, and sometimes angry. But once it became clear that I was saying no as a matter of faith and consistent religious observance of the Sabbath, people were not just accepting, but respectful—even admiring. The Sabbath has been the most public of my Jewish religious observances because it intersects with normal political and governmental scheduling. But I am confident it has not adversely affected my political career, and I know it has not stopped me from fulfilling my governmental responsibilities. It probably has helped in both. Whenever I have the opportunity, I say to young people of all religious persuasions, "Take it from me. You are lucky and blessed to live in a great country at a time when you are not forced to choose between your secular career dreams and ambitions and your observance of religious

faith." Sometimes I think that lesson is one of the most significant contributions I will ever make to my country.

With this understanding, my heart and head are liberated
from compulsive work patterns, and I am ready to stop and
welcome the Sabbath, without hesitation, guilt, or anxiety.

❧ THE SIGNIFICANCE OF GREETING ❧

Welcoming guests to our home shows appreciation and affection for the people we have invited. Greetings at the door
have a ritual aspect. Imagine you have invited friends to your
home for a dinner party. The bell rings and you go to the
door, swinging it open to reveal your friends standing on
the welcome mat. Everyone gives big smiles and maybe ex-
changes hugs and kisses.

You offer an enthusiastic, "Welcome! It's so good to see
you! How have you been?" You help your guests off with
their coats and, gesturing to the couch or chair, ask them to
make themselves comfortable. You might offer refreshments
as well. These are all natural social customs. You don't usually usher guests straight to the dinner table without words
of greeting and connection. Your friends are here to share
companionship with you, not simply to eat. Your welcome
implicitly reminds everyone of that.

If we welcome human guests so elaborately, it makes sense
that in welcoming the spirit of God into our lives and homes
for Shabbat, we should do much more to express our love
and gratitude and to get ourselves in the right spirit for the
time we will spend together in the next twenty-five hours.
Rabbi Joseph Soloveitchik a great modern rabbi and philoso-

pher who lived in Boston and taught generations of rabbis at Yeshiva University in New York, used to point out that on the three seasonal Jewish festivals, when the Israelites traveled to Jerusalem to visit the Temple, "we enter God's palace and He relates to us as a King." But, on the Sabbath, Rabbi Soloveitchik said, "when He comes in our homes as our Guest, He relates to us not as a King but as a Father." And, as a result I would add, we are drawn closer to Him and to one another.

Greeting Shabbat is a beautifully choreographed and absolutely essential feature of Sabbath observance. This greeting is best done in fellowship with others. When we are in Stamford, we gather with others in the synagogue. I drive our car over to the synagogue just before Shabbat comes in, leaving the car there until sundown on Saturday, and walk home after services. When we are in Georgetown, where the walk to *shul* is long, Hadassah and I, and whichever of our children are with us, greet the Sabbath at home. We say and sing the prayers together, which is itself a special family experience.

On Friday evening as we enter the synagogue, the atmosphere is jovial, for when we enter the *shul*, we are entering the heart of Shabbatland. It seems natural, before greeting Shabbat, to greet friends in this special place beyond time. There is a warm feeling of comradery, a reunion with good friends we may not have seen for a week.

Everyone has had a different kind of week, but now we are each cleaned up, dressed up, and ready to share in Shabbat rest, reflection, and regeneration. The mood is decidedly relaxed and convivial. A fellow congregant once told me that this familiarity and cordiality reminded him of the old TV show *Cheers* and the bar where "everybody knows your name" and you know theirs.

At *shul,* I am generally not called Senator but Joe. In public life in Washington, D.C., rank, status, and title matter a great deal. But in the more egalitarian Shabbatland, things are different. Entering the sanctuary, with men and women all dressed up for the Sabbath, you have no way of knowing what anyone else does for a living during the six days of labor. Someone might be a plumber or a grocery store clerk or a doctor or a professor or a senator. Of course, if we are friends, we know each other's businesses and professions. Yet all those distinctions drop away as the Sabbath approaches. In front of God, my title as senator counts for nothing. If I am called to the Torah on Saturday morning, I am called by my traditional Hebrew name, "Yosef Yisrael ben Chanan."

❧ WELCOMING THE SABBATH QUEEN ☙

The initial Friday night synagogue service of the Sabbath is called *Kabbalat Shabbat,* which literally means accepting or receiving the Sabbath. The practices of *Kabbalat Shabbat* were born in Israel in the third century with Rabbi Hanina. The Talmud tells us that at sunset on Friday night, he would robe himself in his finest garments and exclaim to his family and students, "Come and let us go forth and welcome the Sabbath Queen." Another rabbi of about the same period, Rabbi Yannai, had the custom of proclaiming, "Come, O bride! Come, O bride!"

From the simple practices of Rabbi Hanina and Rabbi Yannai almost two millenia ago, there later developed more elaborate, beautiful, and inspirational customs to go with the entrance of the Sabbath Queen. At *Kabbalat Shabbat* we now welcome the Sabbath as if we are the longing bridegroom, going to meet his bride. The Talmud has a lovely spiritual allegory of the Sabbath and its—or rather, her—relationship to the other days of the week. Those other days are, of course, six in number. In a sense each has a partner, since six is an even number. But Shabbat was the odd woman out and complained to God that she had no partner. So God provided her one in the form of, first, the Children of Israel, and then of all who chose to observe the Sabbath.

Like many other observant Jews, I like to read King Solomon's Song of Songs on Friday afternoon, with its richly romantic, sometimes erotic description of love between a man and a woman, representing also the mutual love between God and His creations.

Rabbi Soloveitchik focused not only on the mutual love so powerfully evoked in the Song of Songs but on its persistent note of frustrated longing. In the narrative of the song, the lover hears her beloved knock at the door. But in spite of her long days of yearning, she feels tired and finds excuses for not rising quickly from her bed. When she finally opens the door, he has gone. This is a truly haunting allegory, reminding us that when God knocks on our door, we must not allow distractions to keep us from answering. Each Sabbath, there is that knock at our door. It is up to each of us to choose whether or not to open the door and welcome the King of Kings and the Sabbath Queen.

In the sixteenth century, a highly influential circle of *Kabbalists* arose in northern Israel in the city of Safed, pronounced "*Tz'fat.*" It was in Safed that the greatest mystical community in Jewish history gathered, devoted to the exposition of the mysteries of the Torah. After the expulsion of Jews from Christian Spain in 1492, many Sephardic Jewish refugees found their way to more welcoming Islamic environments, and from there to the Holy Land. Safed, a trading center, became the center of Jewish religious life in Israel during that time.

Among the Jews who migrated to Safed were two brothers-in-law, Solomon Alkabetz and Moses Cordovero, and Rabbi Joseph Karo. Karo is the author of the influential Code of Jewish Law, the *Shulchan Aruch*, which means "Set Table." According to tradition, Karo and Alkabetz were living in Greece when Karo, in the presence and hearing of Alkabetz, received a visitation from an angel who instructed him to depart for Israel. So they went to Safed, which is beautifully situated on a steep, terraced hillside. The community was later led by a charismatic religious genius, Rabbi Isaac Luria, who was known as the *Arizal*, or Holy Lion.

This old city now features a bustling artists' colony, but it remains a center of Jewish spirituality and attracts large numbers of pilgrims and tourists each year. At the bottom of the hill, a dusty ancient cemetery is usually crowded with worshipers, praying and reciting psalms to God before the tombs—many painted blue—of the Kabbalistic saints of the city. The hauntingly attractive, unusually painted synagogues of these mystics are still there, and I have prayed in some of them. One *shul*, populated now by the Breslov Hasidic sect, left a particularly strong impression on me. There is a moment in the Sabbath morning service when we call out the angelic declaration from the book of Isaiah, "Holy, holy, holy is the Lord, of hosts: the whole earth is full of His glory" (6:3). This particular congregation has a tradition of shouting out the words of the angels— "Holy, holy, holy!"—with such enormous volume and passion, like claps of thunder, that it first stunned and then inspired me to join in the loud shouts of faith.

From these holy sages—Rabbis Alkabetz, Cordovero, Karo, and Luria—came today's beautiful practice of greeting the Sabbath Bride. They actually welcomed her outdoors, affirming the angels' declaration that "the whole world is full of His glory." Luria himself taught:

> Go out into an open field and recite, "Come and let us go into the field of holy apple trees in order to welcome the Sabbath Queen." . . . Stand in one place in the field: it is preferable if you are able to do so on a high spot. . . . Turn your face towards the West where the sun sets, and at the very moment that it sets close your eyes and place your left hand upon your chest and your right hand upon your left. Direct your concentration—while in a state of awe and trembling as one who stands in the presence of the King—so as to receive the special holiness of the Sabbath.

The Friday evening service of *Kabbalat Shabbat*, which occurs every week in synagogues around the world, including the two I regularly attend in Connecticut and Washington, captures and transfers the spiritual depth of these luminous personalities of Safed. For me, this service—with its poetic liturgy and compelling hymns—has become one of the most spiritually intense and satisfying times of my religious life.

❧ THE ORDER OF SERVICE ☙

On this journey through Shabbat, there is not time to describe every prayer of the Sabbath. There are other books that do that very well, and I will list some of them in an appendix. But I do want to tell you briefly here about the overall structure of the Friday evening liturgy.

THE OPENING PRAYER

The *Kabbalat Shabbat* service begins with the singing of a passionate prayer composed by another sixteenth century Kabbalist from Safed, Rabbi Elazar Azikri. It is called *Yedid Nefesh*, or "My Soul's Beloved." Rabbi Azikri described his words as "a prayer for union and the desire of love," and that is surely the way I experience it. Here are the words in English of its concluding verses:

> *Reveal Yourself, beloved, and spread over me*
> *the tabernacle of Your peace.*
> *Let the earth shine with Your glory,*
> *let us be overjoyed and rejoice in You.*
> *Hurry, beloved, for the appointed time has come,*
> *and be gracious to me as in the times of old.*

As you can see, these are truly words of passion, devotion, and yearning. They immediately draw us into the depth of Shabbat and are a loving welcome to God as He enters our Shabbat lives.

SONGS TO WELCOME THE SABBATH BRIDE

Next, we say or sing six psalms (95–99, and 29), a custom also begun by the Safed Kabbalists when they dressed in white and went out into the fields to welcome the Sabbath Bride. Each of the six psalms is meant to invoke one of the six days of creation that culminated in the first Shabbat.

The traditional tunes to which some of these psalms are sung have been enlivened lately by newer music composed by, among others, Rabbi Shlomo Carlebach, a charismatic Hasidic rabbi who influenced me in my youth. "Shlomo," as everyone called him, took his guitar in hand and became a wandering minstrel, going everywhere to reach out to people, telling stories of faith, and singing his songs of joy and spirituality. Most of his texts were taken from the Bible, but he wrote his own melodies. As his spirit overflowed, he would break into hand clapping and dancing. He was among the rabbis and other teachers who inspired high school boys and girls at the biannual, week-long Torah Leadership Seminars conducted by Yeshiva University in the 1950s. These seminars were meant specifically for students who, like me, attended public schools instead of Jewish religious or "day" schools. For a week, we would gather at an old camp or Catskill Mountains resort for a total immersion experience in Judaism—and in Shabbat in particular. There was tremendous spirit among us with lots of learning, singing, and traditional circle dancing. I remember myself in one of those endlessly repeating loops, spinning and spinning in a kind of out-of-body experience with Rabbi Sholmo leading us, crying out over and over the words of the prophet Jeremiah, "There will again be heard in the cities of Judah and in the streets of Jerusalem, the sound of joy and the sound of gladness, the voice of the groom and the voice of the bride" (33:10–11).

As I think back today to the passionate, repetitive singing of Jeremiah's prophecy, I am struck by how close we were in time, without knowing it, to the realization of that prophecy. Less than a decade later, in 1967, Israel regained sovereignty over Jerusalem, its ancient political and spiritual capital, including the site of the Holy Temple, where every day you can now hear "the sounds of joy and the sounds of gladness." I think that the thrill of being alive to see Jeremiah's prophecy fulfilled has been experienced as deeply by Christians as by Jews.

An ecstatic Carlebach-style *Kabbalat Shabbat* service can go considerably longer than the typical forty-five minute Friday night service, as worshipers sing and sway and sing and sway. I've experienced a Carlebach service a few times on the broad plaza in front of the Western Wall in Jerusalem, the monumental surviving remnant of the Holy Temple. Today, thousands of Jews gather there on Friday nights in a mingling of many separate prayer services all going on at once, creating what may sound to some like cacophony, but to me seems to fill the plaza with a compelling, inspiring religious energy and togetherness.

The songs of the Sabbath have become one of the most fulfilling ways for me to engage personally in the spirit of the day. I have always enjoyed singing, but the congregational singing of the Sabbath songs has a spiritual force all its own and is a powerful complement to the times of individual, public, or silent prayer during the Sabbath services. Some of the melodies are old and go back not just to my earliest childhood religious experiences, but centuries ago. Others are relatively new, of Carlebach vintage or more recent melodies from modern Israel. Some synagogues have a professional cantor who leads the services. My Georgetown synagogue does not. My Stamford synagogue sometimes does. I love good cantorial singing, but the religious experience works best for me when every worshiper has the opportunity not just to listen to the performance of a cantor, but to join with the cantor or whoever is leading communal song. There is no question that singing the beautiful melodies of the robust Friday night service with my fellow congregants has been one of the ways I make the transition from the six days of labor to the Sabbath of rest, God's day.

A LOVE SONG TO THE SABBATH

These psalms are followed by Rabbi Solomon Alkabetz's own love song to Shabbat, *L'chah Dodi*, which means "Come, my Beloved" and which, tradition holds, was sung by the rabbi and his students as they walked back from the fields through the beautiful streets, up and down the hills of the city of Safed. Like *Yedid Nefesh*, the verses of this song are fully as romantic as the Song of Songs. In many ways, both encapsulate the themes of Solomon's great love poem. The first lines of *L'chah Dodi* are:

> *Come my Beloved, to greet the Bride*
> *let us welcome the Sabbath.*

"My Beloved" is God, and "the Bride" is the Sabbath.

This chorus is sung again after each of the succeeding stanzas, which are about the Sabbath, the holiness of Jerusalem, the promise of redemption, and the coming of the Messiah. "Come, My Beloved" is a hymn of praise, a love song to God and His Sabbath, and an inspiriting call to action.

For the final verse, we turn toward the West, as the Kabbalists in Safed did to see the sun set. But today, as we stand inside the synagogue, we turn to the door of the sanctuary, which is opened to the West, and we sing:

Come in peace, O crown of her husband,
Come with joy and jubilation,
Among the faithful of the treasured people
Enter, O Bride, Enter, O Bride.

With the last words, the congregation bows respectfully from the waist to symbolically welcome the Sabbath bride.

THE *AMIDAH*

After *L'chah Dodi*, the Friday evening *Kabbalat Shabbat* service moves on to the evening prayers at whose center are two major prayers that are in most Jewish religious services: the *Shema Yisrael*, which means "Hear, O Israel," and the *Amidah*, which means "Standing," because it is said standing before God and in silence. Both of these prayers are filled with rich and powerful meanings. So you'll hear about both multiple times throughout this book. I will describe the *Shema* to you in more detail during the Saturday morning service. But let me now briefly introduce the *Amidah*.

The *Amidah* is recited three times every day: at each of the three daily services—evening, morning, and afternoon. On Shabbat, the middle part is altered from service to service (Friday night, Saturday morning, and Saturday afternoon) to reflect the unique ideas and articles of faith we are encouraged to focus on during each phase of the Sabbath.

The *Amidah* is said standing erect with our feet together in the posture that Jewish tradition teaches that the angels adopt when praising their Maker (see Ezekiel 1:7; of the angels carrying the throne of God, the prophet says their legs were straight and together), reminding us that we have a responsibility and capacity to serve and honor God with our words and deeds on Earth, as the angels do in Heaven. The weekday *Amidah* includes nineteen blessings or benedictions, first praising God, then asking Him to help us meet many of our needs, then thanking Him for His kindness. There is a wide listing of human needs prayed for in the *Amidah*—everything from wisdom and good health to good weather and good crops.

The prayers of the Sabbath reflect to us the whole course of divine and human history—past, present, and future. At the Friday evening prayers, at the service that is called *Ma'ariv*, is the primordial creation, the first Sabbath. So in the Friday *Amidah* of *Kabbalat Shabbat* we read the account of creation from Genesis:

> Thus the heavens and the earth were completed, and all their array. With the seventh day God completed the work He had done . . . God blessed the seventh day and declared it holy, because on it, He ceased from all His work he had created to do. (Genesis 2:1–2)

The focus of the Saturday morning prayers is revelation in history. God revealed His will at Mt. Sinai, giving us the Ten Commandments and the Torah, which we read on Shabbat mornings. Finally, the theme of the Saturday afternoon service is the ultimate Sabbath, the Sabbath of Messianic redemption.

When the Friday evening service is over, congregants tend to linger in the sanctuary or lobby a while to socialize informally before going home. The lingering is longer during the winter months when the sun sets earlier and therefore the services start earlier. But even then, the lingering is not too long, because the Sabbath dinner—whose wonderful aromas we have already inhaled—awaits us at home.

❧ SIMPLE BEGINNINGS ❧

⚜ At the beginning of your Sabbath, turn off the TV, computer, cell phone, or all three. Ideally, keep them all turned off for the whole day, but even an evening or afternoon free from electronic media is a blessing. This may be the single best contemporary Simple Beginnings idea there is.

⚜ Consider lighting two candles to welcome the Sabbath as a symbol of your wish that God's light, and the peace that comes with it, should pervade your home for the coming rest day.

⚜ Review the six-day week that's just concluded. Was it a good week for you and your family? What can you do in the coming week to improve your relationships with loved ones, friends, co-workers— and God?

⚜ Too much of our lives are lived indoors. When your Sabbath arrives, if you do not attend a church or synagogue, thank God for the day of rest by going out to the backyard or balcony. If you live in the city, just open a window and breathe in the fresh air or take a walk in a park.

☙ *Chapter Three* ☞

THE SHABBAT MEAL:

HONORING GOD, BLESSING EACH OTHER

Friday Night at Home

Hadassah and I take great pleasure in sharing the Sabbath experience with friends—whether they are observant Jews, nonobservant Jews, or not Jewish. The rabbis suggest that welcoming guests is "greater than greeting the Divine Presence." Their proof text is that Abraham turned from his encounter with God and ran to invite three passing strangers to accept his hospitality (Genesis 18:1–4). The deeper truth is that in greeting humans created in the image of God, we are also greeting our Maker.

Hadassah always sets a beautiful table, with a white tablecloth, our best china and silverware, silver cups for the sacramental wine, and a silver tray with a wooden cutting board for the *challah* bread, which is covered by a beautiful embroidered cloth. The Sabbath candles are still burning brightly. On every other day we eat at the kitchen table, but on Shabbat, we move to the dining room. Observant Jewish families may use their dining room tables more than most people, thanks to the Sabbath and other Jewish holy days.

The atmosphere of a Shabbat dinner is a mixture of spiritual and social, of scripted ritual and informal conviviality, all bathed in a unique and powerful Sabbath tranquility. A sense of calm mysteriously descends on the home and usually on the people in it, who were just a short time before mad with last minute work or Shabbat preparations. One of my favorite memories of the power of the Sabbath to transform is about my friend, the late Richard Holbrooke, the great American diplomat. Dick was always restless and full of energy. Once Hadassah and I invited him and his wife, Kati Marton, to our home for Friday night Shabbat dinner. I must admit, I wondered whether Dick could control his restlessness in a Sabbath setting. As it turned out, that evening was one when voting kept me on Capitol Hill past the beginning of the Sabbath, so I had to walk home. It wasn't raining this time, but it was hot. When I arrived home, I was late for dinner, sweaty, and anxious about keeping everyone waiting. However, when I walked through the door, I instantly felt the amazing calming power of Shabbat. Everyone was sitting around the table, chatting. And there was Dick Holbrooke, just as mellow and relaxed as anyone could be. He was like a different person.

A different person is, in a way, what Friday night beckons us to become. A tradition in the Talmud says that we are blessed with an additional soul on the Sabbath, a gift of added sensitivity, of receptivity and insight. I believe I saw that extra soul in the wonderfully dynamic Richard Holbrooke that memorable Friday night at our Shabbat table.

❧ A PORTABLE SABBATH ❧

While the Sabbath is fundamentally an institution of home and family, it is remarkable how the day and the spirit can be experienced in the most unlikely places—like my Senate office in the Hart Building, a modern and formal structure, generally lacking in a homey feeling. Sometimes when I've had to stay on Capitol Hill on Friday night because there are votes to cast on both Friday night and Saturday that keep me from walking home, Hadassah and I have celebrated Shabbat right there in my office. A few times, I've invited colleagues—Jewish and Christian—to join us for an improvised Sabbath meal, not around a table, but around my Senate desk.

Hadassah spreads out a white tablecloth; I say the sanctification, or blessing, over a cup of kosher wine—a bottle of which I generally keep in the closet behind my desk for just such occasions. We wash our hands and then bless God and break bread together. It may be *challah* or it may only be a couple of matzahs—unleavened bread associated with Passover—that I also keep in that closet.

The most remarkable portable Shabbat we ever celebrated was with Al and Tipper Gore. We had shared a Sabbath or two, as well as a Passover Seder, with the Gores during the 1990s; but the most memorable Friday night we had with them was during the thirty-six-day vote recount that followed the unusual contested election of 2000. On Friday, December 7, the Florida Supreme Court had ruled in our favor and ordered a recount of votes from that state. When he was notified of the ruling, later that Friday afternoon, Vice President Gore called and excitedly told me the news. We were thrilled because we believed that if those votes were recounted, we would win Florida and the election.

It was about fifteen minutes before Shabbat was to begin. Hadassah and I were at our home in Georgetown. The Gores were at the vice president's residence on the grounds of the United States Naval Observatory about a mile away. At the end of the conversation, Al and I said we would talk after sunset on Saturday. As always, I told him that if he needed me during Saturday he should send somebody over to get me, as he had done on the first Sabbath after the election when some of the important decisions about the postelection lawsuits had to be made and he wanted me to be part of the discussion. About five minutes after we ended our phone conversation with mutual "Shabbat Shaloms," the phone rang. It was Al again.

"It's not sunset yet is it?" he asked.

"No," I answered.

"Then why don't you and Hadassah pack up whatever you need and do Sabbath at our house," Al suggested. "We're having a party here to celebrate the court decision, and you should be part of it." I thanked him and said of course we would come. So Hadassah and I gathered up candles, wine, *challah* bread, dinner—everything we needed—and hurried out to the Secret Service limousine that we had during the duration of the campaign.

We made it to the residence just before Shabbos. Most of the key people in the campaign were there, and the atmosphere was jubilant. When we arrived, the Gores greeted us with hugs and high fives. Tipper asked Hadassah what she needed to do first to prepare for the Sabbath, and she said she needed to light the Shabbat candles. Donna Brazile, the campaign manager, and I embraced. She is a very good, smart, able person. She is also a strongly Christian woman who chose a different psalm to read and meditate on each day of the campaign, sharing them with me when we were together. I had seen her earlier that Friday and she told me she was reading Psalm 30, which contains the inspirational verse, "In the evening one lies down weeping, but with dawn—a cry of joy!" When we greeted each other on that Friday night at the vice president's residence, we both just said, "Psalm 30!" and laughed and hugged.

Tipper asked if I needed a quiet place to pray. I said I did and she led Hadassah and me into their living room and closed the doors to give us privacy. I faced east towards Jerusalem, according to the traditional Jewish practice, and prayed the service of *Kabbalat Shabbat*, welcoming the Sabbath, and *Ma'ariv*, the evening prayer. When I finished, I turned around to leave the room and beheld a surprising backdrop for my Sabbath prayers, which I somehow hadn't noticed on coming into the room. There behind me, all lit up and beautifully decorated, was the Gores' Christmas tree. It was a very ecumenical Shabbat.

Hadassah and I then joined the crowd in celebration of the Florida court decision. In time, most of them left to go home or out to continue the celebration at a local restaurant. Only a few, including Donna Brazile, remained for dinner with the Gores and Hadassah and me. They asked us what we normally do at home on Friday night and said they hoped we would let them experience it with us; and so we led our friends through the blessings and songs of a Shabbat dinner.

Tipper asked Hadassah and me if she was correct that on the Sabbath we don't use cell phones or BlackBerries except in case of an emergency. When we said yes, she said, "Al, let's turn off our electronics. If anyone really needs us, they'll know how to get us."

It was such a joyous, peaceful, and hopeful dinner. When we were done and it was time to leave, Al asked if we were going to walk home. We said yes, and he and Tipper said they would accompany us. We resisted, but they persisted; and so on that beautiful December night, the four of us—with the Secret Service discreetly walking behind and security cars ahead and behind—walked out their back gate onto Wisconsin Avenue, down the avenue, and then over to our house near Georgetown University—a little more than a mile away.

It was a night when we felt at the door of history and also very close to these two fine people. Sometimes passersby in cars would recognize us and honk their horns and shout out happily. When we got to our house, we hugged and said goodnight and Shabbat Shalom to each other, and the Gores got in their limousine and were driven home.

❧ THE RITUALS OF THE SHABBAT TABLE ☙

Now that I've shared some stories about portable Shabbats we have observed, I want to tell you about the short service at our table that precedes dinner. The focus on Friday night is honoring God as Creator, but also on blessing each other.

A BLESSING FOR OUR CHILDREN

I begin by blessing our children (and now their spouses, whom we consider to be our children) and our grandchildren. When our kids were growing up, and even now when they are visiting us for Shabbat, I stand next to each of them, no matter their age, put my hands on their shoulders or head, recite the traditional blessing, and kiss them. When they are not with us at the Shabbat dinner table, Hadassah and I "beam" our blessing to them, by something like a spiritual satellite, from wherever we are to wherever they are, naming each in turn and reminding ourselves where they and their spouses and children are that Friday night—whether it's New York, Atlanta, Israel, or somewhere else.

For our sons, tradition calls us to begin the blessing saying: "May God make you like Ephraim and like Manasseh" (Genesis 48:20). Ephraim and Manasseh were Joseph's sons, born in Egypt where their father was the viceroy under Pharaoh. Joseph's father, the patriarch Jacob, blessed Joseph with the wish that future generations should bless their own sons this way. He invoked Ephraim and Manasseh specifically because unlike earlier generations of Jacob's family, going back to Abraham, that were filled with strife between brothers, Ephraim and Manasseh got along well together. We pray for the same for our children. Our daughters are blessed in the name of the biblical matriarchs—Sarah, Rebecca, Rachel, and Leah—in the hope that they will emulate the characteristics of those great women. The traditional words of blessing that follow for sons and daughters are those which the high priest Aaron, brother of Moses, spoke in blessing the entire Jewish people and which are familiar to so many because they are still said in churches and synagogues throughout the world today:

May the Lord bless you and protect you. May the Lord make His face shine on you and be gracious to you. May the Lord turn His face to you and grant you peace. (Numbers 6:24–26)

Of all the things that observant Jews do on the Sabbath, which anyone of any faith could and should do, I would put blessing your family high on the list. It is a priceless moment of connection and love between parent and child. It's a statement that no matter what has happened during the week, the parent feels blessed to have that child and asks God's blessing on that son or daughter. As a parent, you know that weeks can go by when you think of your children less as blessings and more as problems to be solved. Any parent knows what I'm talking about, no matter the age of the child. Stopping to bless our children once a week makes us pause to appreciate how blessed we are to have them in the first place and reminds them of the love we feel for them. Our children are truly precious gifts from the Holy One.

WELCOMING THE SABBATH ANGELS OF PEACE

In the Sabbath table hymn *Shalom Aleichem* ("Peace Upon You"), we next welcome the angels of the Sabbath who will be with us for the Sabbath day and bid farewell to the angels of the ordinary week, who depart from us on Friday night. There is a changing of the angelic guard, like the one Jacob saw, according to tradition, on leaving the land of Israel and beholding the famous ladder with angels going up and down. A group of angels accompanied him when he journeyed in the Holy Land, and a different group—workday angels, you might say—when he ventured outside the land of Israel.

"Bless me with peace," we ask in this song, "angels of

peace, angels of the Most High, from the supreme King of Kings, the Holy One, blessed be He."

A BLESSING FOR OUR WIVES

Next we turn to our wives and sing a song of praise, gratitude, and blessing that is taken from the last chapter in the book of Proverbs. It is called *Aishet Chayil*, the "Woman of Valor," and by tradition it is thought to have been sung originally by the patriarch Abraham when he was paying tribute to his own beloved wife, Sarah. I will not reproduce it all here, but take a look at the text if you get a moment (Proverbs 31:10–31). It's an impressively dynamic picture of a wife who is far from the stereotype of women from ancient times as retiring and shy, staying in the background as their husbands go about in the world. The woman of Proverbs 31 not only cares for her family but is an entrepreneur, buying and selling land, trading in her own handiworks, giving to charity, and teaching the "Torah of kindness" to others. In fact, her husband seems like a passive figure by comparison, sitting in the gates—the judicial and administrative centers in biblical times—with the elders of the land.

Aishet Chayil is a tribute that a husband sings to his wife and one that I feel very deeply as I sing it to Hadassah and our daughters.

THE EMPOWERMENT OF BLESSING

The essential spirit of the Sabbath blessing is gratitude for our families and a profound acknowledgment that our gratitude must be to God for the gifts He has given us. But the blessings of spouse and children at the Sabbath table are also personally empowering because they remind us that any one of us can and should bless others. This may seem audacious or awkward to some people. They may ask: Isn't the power to bless limited to special people? Receiving a blessing from a saint or a clergyman makes sense. But from a senator? Or from anyone who, like me, is not a saint? The truth is, any one of us has the power to bless others by our words and actions. I've been blessed many times by strangers. Literally blessed. When I was running for vice president in 2000, many people would approach me and offer a blessing, which I always gratefully accepted.

A Secret Service agent who traveled with me that year and went with me through the diverse crowds that you meet in an American political campaign told me, "I never heard so many people say 'God bless you!' to a national candidate before." I wonder if that was because they knew I was religious and therefore appreciated their blessings.

So it may be that the most uplifting aspect of all the blessing we do at the Friday night Shabbat table is the spiritual empowerment that allows us to give blessings in the first place. Despite my being no saint, the Sabbath tells me that I am—like Aaron, the high priest—a priest in my own right. Every human being is capable of priesthood and blessing in this way. The Bible calls the children of Israel a "kingdom of priests" (Exodus 19:6), a people with a God-given mission to bless, uplift, and serve others. But, of course, that isn't only true of Jews. Every human being has a priestly mission in the world, which is why we can bless others with our words and deeds.

Once during a Thanksgiving visit I made to a soup kitchen, a homeless man came over, shook my hand, and asked, "Senator, would it be okay if I blessed you?" Frankly, I was initially surprised, but what he said reminded me of a great truth: this homeless, hungry man in tattered clothes had as much God-given capacity to bless me as I did to bless him, and what was most important is that he knew that to be the truth.

A BLESSING FOR THE WINE

The Sabbath empowers us to share a vital lesson with the world, which is highlighted by the ritual of *Kiddush*, the sanctification of the Sabbath that is said at the Shabbat table service over a cup of wine before dinner.

Kiddush is another love song to the Sabbath. Why is it said over wine? In the great Temple in Jerusalem, wine libations accompanied the singing of psalms of praise to God by the Levites, who were assistants to the priests. Wine is a stimulant to our praise and is described in the Bible as "wine that makes glad the heart of man" (Psalm 104:15). Wine can help us to express our appreciation and love, whether of God, our family, or of our spouse. The root of the word *Kiddush* is *kadosh*, or holy. The *Kiddush* is not about celebrating drunkenness from wine. It is about sanctifying the wine and enjoying it in moderation.

The words of the *Kiddush* speak first of the creation of the world—the big focus of every Shabbat. We sing the verses from Genesis 2: "Then the heavens and the earth were completed, and all their array. With the seventh day, God completed the work He had done." We then say a blessing in thanks for wine: "Blessed are You, Lord our God, King of the universe, Who creates the fruit of the vine." Finally we bless God directly for the gift of the Sabbath, "a remembrance of the work of creation" and a "heritage" bequeathed to us by Him, concluding, "Blessed are You, Lord, Who sanctifies the Sabbath."

WASHING HANDS

After the *Kiddush* and before the prayer over the *challah* bread, we wash our hands but not for hygienic purposes. The washing of the hands is a partial immersion—a limited form of the total immersion in life-giving water which is a traditional Jewish rebirth ritual. Of course, Christians also immerse in baptismal waters as a ritual of spiritual rebirth. Washing our hands uplifts what might be a mundane activity—feeding ourselves—to a higher spiritual level. In fact, the Hebrew phrase for washing hands, *netilat yadayim*, literally means lifting or taking. In other words, the goal of the washing is not cleanliness, but sanctifying our eating, reminding us that we should eat to live, not live to eat. At the sink, we use a two-handled washing cup to pour water over our hands—twice over the right, twice over the left—and as we dry our hands with a towel, we say the Hebrew blessing, "Blessed are you Lord our God, King of the universe, who commanded us concerning the washing of hands." We don't speak after that blessing, until we bless God and eat the bread, to emphasize that the washing is preparation for breaking bread, and we don't want worldly conversation to interrupt these holy acts.

A BLESSING OVER BREAD

Everyone returns to the table, and the leader of the meal thanks God for our nourishment: "Blessed are you Lord our God, King of the universe, who brings forth bread from the earth." For Roman Catholics especially, this washing of hands, eating bread, and drinking wine will probably remind you of the Mass. That, of course, is not coincidental because the Mass reenacts the Last Supper, which was a Passover Seder at which Jesus surely said the traditional prayers over the wine and matzah.

At our Shabbat table, the head of the household takes up not one loaf of bread but two. Why two? Because the loaves are meant to recall the mysterious manna that appeared daily in the fields to sustain the Israelites during their forty years in the desert. The manna is held by some rabbis to be the same food that angels consume—the very "glow of God's presence"—but given a material aspect so that human beings could recognize and grasp it. In the desert, manna fell every day but Saturday. On Friday, the manna appeared miraculously in a double portion. God instructed the Israelites not to go out into the wilderness to gather manna on Saturday, because it would not be there and because gathering food would violate the Sabbath rest. Instead, they should bake or cook it however they liked before Friday night, since again, cooking would disturb the Sabbath atmosphere. It was a lesson in faith. God was telling them, as He tells us, that we can stop our laboring for a day without fear of suffering want or deprivation. As the double loaves remind us, God will take care of us.

In sum, the ritual aspect of the Friday night meal is actually quite brief—the blessing of our children and wives, the hymn welcoming the Sabbath Angels of Peace, the prayer over wine, the washing of the hands, and the blessing over the bread. It's time now to eat, drink, talk, and enjoy each other and the atmosphere of warmth and peace. I try to share a thought from the Bible at the meal. We also sing Sabbath songs to add to the celebratory mood, but the dinner is otherwise not a scripted event. Our social, sensual, and intellectual enjoyment is no less a part of Shabbat than the formal blessings.

✥ THOUGHTS SHARED AROUND THE SABBATH TABLE ✥

When our family and friends sit comfortably around the Sabbath table—enjoying a glass of wine, the delicious meal Hadassah has prepared, and each other's fellowship—we usually also share a few thoughts and stories about the Sabbath. So, that is what I will do now.

GOD AS CREATOR

Standing for the *Kiddush* prayer that is said over the wine is one of the ways we give public testimony that the world has a Creator. We stand for *Kiddush* because in Jewish law, witnesses before the court are required to stand while giving their testimony. In saying *Kiddush*, we are standing to publicly proclaim that the world has a Creator.

It can be strangely controversial to stand up and testify to the existence of our Creator. Once when I was on *Meet the Press* with the late, great Tim Russert and a panel of people of different religions, I described myself as a creationist. Afterward, one of my staff members pleaded with me never to use such a loaded word again. I told them that since I believe in God, the Creator of Heaven and Earth, I thought it was an accurate self-description, and I would use it again when appropriate.

I know that human existence is seen by some as an accident, the product of blindly churning natural forces, an unguided process without direction or meaning. That viewpoint can leave people without a guiding compass. The Sabbath, in contrast, offers a way to help us focus with hope on eternal truths and values. The Bible teaches that this world was intentionally created with purpose, order, and moral standards. The rabbis teach that the Sabbath was the culmination of God's creative activity. And so the Sabbath is set aside as a time of rest when people can express their appreciation to God for His creation and their lives, when they can use their spiritual powers to come closer to each other and to God. Remembering that there is a Creator who brought the universe into existence, who purposefully shaped the endless diversity of life, and rested on a cosmic Sabbath sets the standards for us to live our lives, striving to imitate God's behavior and fill our own lives with meaning, joy, and purpose. Sabbath observance is a great way to affirm and strengthen that belief one day every week.

AN ETERNAL COVENANT

The Sabbath is not just a day we observe religiously. It is also a covenant: "Wherefore the children of Israel shall keep the Sabbath, to observe the Sabbath throughout their generations, for a perpetual covenant" (Exodus 31:16). A covenant is a mutual agreement—a partnership between the covenanters. The Shabbat covenant reminds us that we have been blessed to be invited by God to become partners in the divine Creation and that we have been called to raise up the world and fix it. It is the nature of covenants that they change our status when we enter into them. The Bible defines how our status can be changed in the first covenant—circumcision. God originally gave it to Abraham, saying "Thou shalt keep My covenant therefore, thou, and thy seed after thee in their generations" (Genesis 17:9). The Hebrew word that is routinely used to mean circumcision, *brit*, literally means "covenant." Just as a Jewish boy enters the covenant of Abraham on the eighth day of his life and is changed by it to a new status, so a Sabbath observer renews the covenant of the Sabbath with God every weekend and also changes his or her status.

THE SABBATH IS FOR EVERYONE

I want to stress again that—as important as Sabbath observance has been in keeping the Jewish people alive over the centuries—the Sabbath was given as a gift from God to everyone. On the other hand, eating kosher food and putting on *tefillin* to pray in the morning are more unique to the Jewish experience. (*Tefillin*, also called phylacteries in English, are a pair of black leather boxes containing parchment with handwritten scriptural passages, which are worn on the head and arm.) Let me tell you a story that illustrates the difference.

Once during the 1990s, John McCain and I were on an airplane traveling to Bosnia to visit our troops as part of a senatorial delegation, and he was sleeping in the seat across the aisle from mine. I was awakened by the sunlight and put on my *tefillin* and a prayer shawl to say my morning prayers. I noticed John open his eyes for a moment and look at me, then close them again. Then, doing a double take, his eyes opened wide.

"Where am I? What is going on!" he blurted out

"Johnny," I said, "I'm just saying my morning prayers." I explained briefly about the *tefillin* and prayer shawl, and he responded, "Oh good, for a moment there, Joey, I thought I'd died and gone to heaven."

I could not help but say: "That says a lot about what kind of person you are, my friend: you think when you get to heaven you're going to see a lot of Jews praying!"

John's response, in any event, shows that putting on *tefillin* is something unfamiliar to most people.

The Sabbath is very different. The Sabbath is for everybody, and it is particularly and deeply *American*. I don't get that kind of startled response from John to my Sabbath observance when we travel together, because the Sabbath idea is familiar to him and most people. In fact, John has become very familiar with the quirks and extra demands of traveling with a Sabbath-observant Jew over the years and seems to enjoy our mad dashes to get me to foreign destinations before sundown on Friday; he takes pleasure in kidding me about them. He's not the only one. Al Gore told me before the election of 2000 that if we won, he'd consider restoring Sunday as a more traditional Sabbath in his life and in the White House. He joked about letting me "run the store" on Sunday so he could observe the Sabbath in his way, while he would "run the store" on Saturday while I was observing Shabbat.

SABBATH OBSERVANCE IN AMERICAN HISTORY

There is, in fact, a strong precedent for an American president taking Sunday "off." The Sabbath was long a factor in American presidential politics and governance. In the 1828 election, notorious for its excess of mudslinging, partisans of Andrew Jackson accused John Quincy Adams of being a Sabbath breaker. Zachary Taylor refused to be inaugurated on a Sunday because it was the Sabbath. Millard Fillmore put a stop to the custom of allowing visitors with business to come to the White House on Sunday. He instructed his staff that his Sabbath rest wasn't to be disturbed and cited both the spiritual and health benefits of the practice. Franklin Pierce conducted no business on the Sabbath and would not even allow the mail to be opened.

In the James K. Polk White House, Mrs. Polk was known as a strict Sabbath enforcer. Polk himself only saw official visitors on Sunday when very urgent matters were at stake—like avoiding war with Great Britain over the disputed Oregon Territory. Presidents also took care about the Sabbath observance of their subordinates, even in wartime. During the Civil War and the First World War respectively, presidents Lincoln and Wilson, the latter a strict, Sabbath-observant Presbyterian, issued general orders to Army and Navy personnel that the Sabbath rest be respected as far as it was practical. Teddy Roosevelt, probably the greatest outdoorsman ever to inhabit the White House, would not hunt or fish on Sunday.

In addition to the presidents who observed the Sabbath, large numbers of the American public observed it also. Alexis de Tocqueville, the French aristocrat who toured America in 1831, was struck by the religiosity of the American people, which he saw as a key precondition for liberty. He especially noticed the prevalence of Sabbath observance, saying that even in a "great American city" a pervasive calm and quiet descended on Saturday night and continued through Sunday: "If you go through the streets at the hour when you would expect grown-up people to be going to their businesses, and young ones to their pleasures, you will find yourself in profound solitude." Only on Monday at daybreak did the city wake up.

Detailed laws against Sabbath breaking existed in most states. Though not always strictly enforced, these "blue laws" expressed the country's faith that something of community-wide importance was at stake in respecting the Sabbath. In the colonies and later in the states—in places as diverse as

Virginia, Maryland, and New York—you could be fined as much as twenty or thirty dollars for traveling, doing business, hunting, attending a horse race, or, in New York State, "frequenting tippling houses"—that is, going to bars—on Sunday. Some historians say the laws were called "blue" because of the color of the paper they were first printed on in my home state of Connecticut in 1665.

As state attorney general in Connecticut in the 1980s, I had the privilege to fight to preserve the last vestiges of those laws. On one occasion I argued a case before the U.S. Supreme Court that was at the intersection of the Sabbath and the Constitution. The 1984 case *Estate of Thornton v. Caldor, Inc.* centered on a Christian man, Donald Thornton, who worked for a department store chain and who, as a Presbyterian, wanted to take Sunday off. After Connecticut's blue laws were repealed, the store's management made it hard for him to do this. The question was whether the state law, which required employers to continue to accommodate the religious desire of employees who did not want to work on Sunday, violated the First Amendment prohibition against "establishing religion." I'm sorry to say that the court ruled for Caldor against Donald Thornton.

Today, across the country, blue laws have been almost entirely dismantled. Rare is the large business that closes on Sunday. I know of only a couple of national chains that do so. One is the fast-food chicken restaurant called Chick-fil-A, founded by a devout Christian, Truett Cathy. Another is Hobby Lobby, founded by David Green. God bless them and any others who honor and guard the Sabbath by closing their businesses.

My point in this brief historical recollection is that rediscovering and reclaiming the Sabbath means reclaiming part of our inheritance as Americans. I am not saying we should bring back the old blue laws, but I do not hesitate to say to every American I can that I hope you will rediscover the Sabbath in a way that is meaningful for you.

❧ A SWEET FINISH ❧

As we conclude our Friday-evening discussion and meal, we sing some *zemirot*, songs of praise and celebration that are a highlight of each of the three Sabbath meals. These hymns and poetry are sung to a variety of melodies picked up along the journey of Jewish history—Spanish, German, Eastern European, American and now Israeli.

Here is a stanza from one of my Friday night favorites, *Tzur Mishelo*:

> *He feeds His world—our Shepherd, our Father,*
> *we have eaten of His bread, His wine we have drunk.*
> *So let us thank His name, let us praise Him with our*
> *   mouths,*
> *saying, singing: None is Holy like the Lord.*

We conclude with the grace after the meal, called *Bentsching*, for "Blessing" in Yiddish or *Birkat Hamazon*, for "Blessing for Nourishment" in Hebrew.

This grace is a series of blessings sung to all manner of music, but ordained in the Bible: "When thou hast eaten and art replete, then thou shalt bless the Lord thy God" (Deuteronomy 8:10). The opening words are: "Blessed are You, Lord our God, King of the Universe, who in His goodness feeds the whole world with grace, kindness and compassion. He gives food to all living things, for His kindness is forever."

The Sabbath dinner is formally over, but our pleasure isn't. There is one *mitzvah* or commandment, yet to be fulfilled this Friday night—a particularly special one that God gave to husbands and wives to enjoy together. We have read some passionate poetry. We have relaxed with a little wine. The dining room table was candlelit. It's almost a "date" atmosphere that God and the rabbis have engineered. In the following chapter, I'll elaborate on what happens next, as far as the limits of good taste and privacy allow.

❧ SIMPLE BEGINNINGS ❧

- Before sitting down to your Sabbath meal, bless your children with whatever blessing seems appropriate. Connect to your children physically, placing your hands on their head or shoulders. If your children are off on their own, think of them and ask God to bless them wherever they may be.

- Thank God for your food by saying grace, either from a prepared text or by speaking from your heart. Consider thanking God *after* you eat as well as before.

- Sing with your family or even by yourself. The Sabbath is the ideal time for music—not the electronically generated kind but the warm words and tunes of hymns to God that only human beings can bring forth from themselves.

- The Sabbath is our opportunity to reflect on the way God's creative purpose and design are reflected in the world around us. Meditate on God's creation of life and nature and the entire cosmos—not as an abstract idea disconnected from our daily reality but as an observable fact: "The heavens declare the glory of God, and the firmament proclaims His handiwork" (Psalm 19:1).

Chapter Four

SUNSET, SUNRISE:

INTIMACY, HUMAN AND DIVINE

Friday Night & Saturday Morning

A while ago, a national news magazine did a cover story on marriage in America and reported that between 15 and 20 percent of married couples have sexual relations with each other fewer than ten times a year. In marriages that incorporate the Sabbath as traditionally observed, such infrequent intimacy would be rare because it would be considered irreligious.

That is why one afternoon in Miami during the 2000 campaign, I inadvertently made Hadassah blush in public. It was a Friday afternoon, and she and I had been separated from each other all week while we each traveled and campaigned for the Gore–Lieberman ticket. We planned to spend Shabbat together in a South Florida hotel, but first there would be a big Friday-afternoon rally in Miami.

When I came on stage and saw her, she really looked beautiful. "Oh, I haven't seen Hadassah all week," I said, hamming it up for the audience, "I can't wait to spend the Sabbath with her." I gave her a big kiss. The crowd ooed and aahed and clapped. She smiled and blushed, and the photographers got a wonderful picture of us together. There might even have been some observant Jews present in the crowd that afternoon who understood the romantically charged nature of Friday night; and, therefore, why Hadassah was blushing so deeply.

In contemporary society, people are so frantically busy and stressed out, it's no wonder that marital intimacy has suffered as a result. The Torah and the rabbis who interpreted it appear to have foreseen this, and so Shabbat gives couples an extra push to make sure they come together at least once a week. I hasten to emphasize: that's a minimum, not a maximum.

❧ A BRILLIANT COMMANDMENT ☙

That sexual relations between married couples should be required on the Sabbath makes good sense in ways that are practical, religious, and even mystical. Much of the staging of Friday night is conducive to romance: the passionate Song of Songs that is read, the wine, the candles, the set table, everyone dressed up and looking their best yet relaxed and unhurried. It's a brilliantly conceived recipe for reunion.

The real brilliance, though, may be that for the Sabbath observant, Shabbat is not an option but a commandment. So, too, is Shabbat intimacy. It's easy for couples to find themselves letting other things get in the way of being together—seemingly *urgent* things, like staying late at the office or answering email, that in reality aren't all that important.

Sometimes marriage and marital intimacy need the ritualized and obligatory rules that Shabbat brings.

"If thou . . . call the Sabbath a delight," says the prophet Isaiah, "then thou shalt delight thyself in the Lord" (58:13–14). This is not just an idle promise. The rabbis asked themselves what "delight" the prophet was referring to. In answer, they cited the ancient tradition that it was sexual relations, among other delights of Shabbat, that Isaiah had in mind.

A commentary on religious law, the *Mishnah Berurah*, reminds husbands to be careful not to let their fulfillment of this commandment slip. On the eve of the Sabbath, it advises, a man should be scrupulous to show his wife extra affection and avoid quarreling. The rabbis even had an opinion about which foods contribute to sexual desire! They recommended roasted garlic and cooked but unsalted lentils.

How well these foods really work, I don't know. But the point is, husbands and wives should not treat being intimate with each other as a casual thing, dependent on whim, mood, or convenience. As with Shabbat in general, we need to give the pleasures of life, which sustain life, the care and priority they deserve.

❧ A REFLECTION ON OUR INTIMACY WITH GOD ❧

Beyond the physical connection, there is a deeper link between marital sex and Shabbat. The relationship between spouses is an earthly reflection of the intimate relationship between humans and our God. In fact, the word *intimate* that describes the relationship between husband and wife is often used in both Jewish and Christian communities to describe the loving relationship between God and humans.

In the Bible, God makes clear his desire for the love of His children.

The tabernacle, or tent, where the Children of Israel worshiped Him in the desert after they left Egypt was called, in Hebrew, the *Ohel Mo'ed*, meaning the Tent of Rendezvous. The Tabernacle was later given a permanent architectural form as Solomon's great Temple in Jerusalem. Its innermost sanctum, the Holy of Holies, is sometimes called the *zevul*. Rabbi Joseph B. Soloveitchik has pointed out that the word *zevul* is also used to designate the most intimate and private room in the home, where husband and wife sleep with and enjoy each other.

God and the Israelites entered into their "marital" relationship at the foot of Mt. Sinai. According to Rabbi Soloveitchik, the reason Moses smashed the first tablets of the Ten Commandments was because they represented a legal gift, like a wedding ring, that would have signified the formal enactment of the marriage. When Moses was bringing the tablets down the side of the mountain, he was horrified to see the Israelites worshiping the Golden Calf. If the marriage had already taken place, their idol worship would have been an act of spiritual adultery. To save his fellow Israelites from having such a grievous sin on their souls, Rabbi Soloveitchik taught, Moses broke the tablets and thus kept the marriage from being finalized then. Later, God and the Israelites were spiritually "married" after the Israelites repented and God forgave them for their idolatry.

The Sabbath is like a weekly reenactment of that marriage—an anniversary day celebrated fifty-two times a year.

The marital chamber is the most private in the home, and so our tour of Shabbatland must stop at our bedroom door, to be taken up again some hours later. As they say in the movies, we'll "cut to" a morning scene.

❧ SHABBAT MORNING— PEACEFUL MOMENTS AT HOME ☙

The sun has risen in Washington or Stamford and light creeps through the windows. It is Saturday morning—Shabbat morning.

Almost everything about Shabbat is different from the other six days. But one thing that doesn't change is the first words I say when I wake up on Saturday morning. I learned them when I was a young child at religious school and have said them every morning of my life since. The words are a prayer called by its first two words in Hebrew, *Modeh Ani*. It is a very short prayer: "I gratefully thank You, living and eternal King, for giving me back my soul in mercy. Great is your faithfulness." That's it, just those few words, but they make big statements about life and faith, first thing every morning.

The Code of Jewish Law urges us to wake up every morning with gratitude to God and with a "lion-like resolve" to serve our Creator.

I cannot say that I awake every morning like a lion, but I can tell you that I have never found a better way to start every day than by thanking God for sustaining my soul in my body and giving me all the opportunities of a new day of life.

While the first words I speak are the same on Shabbat as on every other day, the next thing I do is different.

One of my favorite responsibilities in our house (Hadassah might say it is one of the only responsibilities I have in the house) is to brew the coffee she and I drink each morning. But never on Saturday.

For me, among the special tastes of Shabbat is the taste of instant coffee. You might think of instant as inferior to the brewed variety. And I would agree. But on Shabbat its advantage is that it is different. When Hadassah and I get up every other day of the week, I brew coffee in our coffee maker. On Shabbat, I cannot turn on the coffee maker so we have instant coffee made with the water I preboiled on Friday afternoon and kept hot in the electric urn.

And so this has become for me one of the unique tastes of Shabbat. On other days of the week, my breakfast, at the suggestion of my friend Dr. Nicholas Perricone, is a can of high quality wild Pacific salmon. On the Sabbath, we have a different, slightly less disciplined breakfast, some cereal with milk, or cookies, or yogurt with fruit, or *babka*, a rich cake of Eastern European origins heavily layered with chocolate or cinnamon. Like Proust's madeleine, these foods at breakfast immediately conjure up Shabbat for me.

The other six mornings of the week are usually rushed and full of activities: exercising, praying, and running off to work. I still enjoy the old-fashioned pleasure of reading newspapers, but on most mornings I must skim the papers and quickly check the news digests on my Kindle or my BlackBerry. On Shabbat, the BlackBerry and Kindle are off limits, and Hadassah and I have time to linger over the papers. In the spring and summer, we open the doors and take our coffee out to the patio in Washington or the balcony in Stamford and enjoy the sights and sounds of the outdoors. We talk about what we are reading in the papers or about things that happened during the week that we didn't have time to share. These are small but significant pleasures.

On Shabbat, I have a personal custom of never wearing a wristwatch. I don't wear a watch so I won't keep looking at it to check the time, as I do on the other six days. It is my personal way of reminding myself that Shabbat is beyond the normal weekday pressures of time; yet paradoxically, the Sabbath is also highly ordered—particularly by the natural setting, rising, and setting of the sun.

In fact, the concept of appointed times is essential to Judaism. Shabbat comes every week at a very precisely defined moment determined by the time the sun sets. It may be at 5:16 or 6:45 or 7:22 p.m. on Friday. Check the weather page in your local newspaper—with candle lighting time precisely eighteen minutes before sunset (a rabbinically ordained buffer zone so the observant person will not wait until the last minute and maybe miss the deadline). The number eighteen is the equivalent of the Hebrew letters of the word *chai*, (or "life"). Being late is not an option.

⚘ SHABBAT MORNING— THE INTIMACY OF PRAYER SERVICE ⚘

Each synagogue decides communally when prayers begin on Saturday morning, a set time from week to week, and that's when you get there. At many synagogues, it's 9:00 a.m., with the prayer service (the *davening*, in Yiddish) lasting about three hours. In the two *shuls* where I most often pray, in Washington and Stamford, there's an early service that I enjoy attending because it's less formal, smaller, and quicker (it only goes for *two* hours), so you get done earlier and can thus enjoy more of the day of rest.

More people attend the Saturday morning prayer service than any other during the week—it's a special time of social interaction, and of intimacy. As Hadassah and I walk from home to synagogue, either by way of the Georgetown University campus if we're in Washington for Shabbat or through the streets of Stamford in Connecticut, we see friends and neighbors on their way to *shul*. We greet each other amiably. People ask how our family is, how our week was, or what's new in our lives.

Attendance at synagogue on Saturday morning is a major weekly reunion of those of us who dwell in Shabbatland. Some of the social interaction continues even after we are in synagogue, and sometimes that leads to talking during the service. I have never seen anything like it in non-Orthodox Jewish congregations or non-Jewish houses of worship. While most of the time is spent praying, people sometimes talk during parts of the service when Jewish law and the prayer book are less stringent about *not* talking. For example, once the synagogue service begins on Saturday morning, there is only prayer, no side-conversations for about thirty-five or forty minutes. During the two major prayers (the *Shema* and *Amidah*) and the reading of the Torah, there is total focus on the prayers and reading. But after those, and in between, there tends to be some unrelated conversation, social or serious.

Strictly speaking, this is not consistent with Jewish law. The major legal code, the *Shulchan Aruch*, is clear that our time in synagogue is for praying, not for chatting. But the inability to meet that standard is not just contemporary. There are records from as long ago as the Middle Ages of rabbis instructing their congregations about the importance of not talking during prayers, just as some of today's rabbis regularly have to shush the members of their synagogues. This tendency to socialize between intense prayer times may be a by-product of the combination of communal and individual prayer in the traditional Jewish service. Some prayers are sung, more or less in unison. But many of the prayers are recited quietly or loudly by each individual in what may seem to a visitor like a cacophony, but to me feels like a personal conversation with God in the midst of a congregation of people who are all doing the same. The net effect—though not orderly—is comforting, communal, and personal. It may also encourage the relaxed conversation that occurs during other less intense parts of the service.

There are two other more mundane causes for the un-prayerful talk in synagogue. One is that we like each other, and the other is that the Shabbat morning service is awfully long. One of my fellow congregants in Stamford, Bill Meyers, has a card he carries in his pocket and when someone tries to talk to him while he is praying, he shows it to them. It says, "Please forgive me for not responding. I'm talking to God."

I mentioned earlier that I have a friend who says that when he enters the synagogue on Friday night, it feels like the bar on the TV show *Cheers*. Arriving at *shul* sometimes also feels to me like I am stepping into a modern version of Anatevka, the fictional small town in Russia where the musical *Fiddler on the Roof* took place. The cast of characters has a small-town feel. In Anatevka, you had Tevye the milkman, Lazer Wolf the butcher, and Matil the tailor—their daily lives all woven intimately together. In my synagogues today, we have Mark the doctor, Jim the journalist, and Joe the senator. Some of these friendships extend to professional consultations. In synagogue, Joe might complain to Mark of a pain in his knee, to which Mark replies by complaining to Joe about Joe's vote on the Iraq war.

And there can be feuds. Jim the journalist, who used to write very positively about Joe, has lately been writing some things about Joe that Joe thinks are unfair. Now instead of greeting each other with a hearty "Good *Shabbos!*" when they pass on the stairs, Joe and Jim merely nod their hellos. As you will recall, things like this happened in Anatevka too.

In *Fiddler on the Roof*, the town had its eccentric personalities—just like our synagogue. The fiddler himself, perched on rooftops and playing his violin, would be one of them. In my Washington synagogue, we have a special member— Sholom Dovid Winograd—who would have easily fit into Anatevka. Sholom Dovid has a beard and wears a black hat and black silk coat in synagogue and is known for his religious devotion, offbeat personality, and superb wit. During my 2000 vice presidential campaign, he initially worried the Secret Service agents who were assigned to my protective detail. They were not prepared for a custom that he and I have had for more than fifteen years now. At a certain point in the Saturday morning service when the ark is opened so we can return the Torah we have read and we are singing a song which means "The Torah is a tree of life to those who uphold it," Sholom Dovid always comes up to me and throws an arm around my shoulder. Together, we sway back and forth as we sing the song of praise to God. We are the only two people doing this in the synagogue.

Someone as "unconventional" as Sholom Dovid getting so close to a vice presidential candidate unsettles Secret Service agents. Before things could get really uncomfortable for everyone, I advised them it was all right. He was a friend and safe.

I once asked him why he does this every Shabbat, and he answered quickly, directly, and surprisingly, "*Ahavas Yisrael*"—the love of Israel.

I think that was his way of saying that for him, as for many others, the synagogue is like a large extended family or a small town with diverse members who are nonetheless bound together in a community. People care about and care for each other. Of course this isn't unique to Jews. I have seen the same in Christian churches, and I assume it is true in other religions as well. In fact, as you probably know, communal worship is statistically associated with better health and longer lives. Plenty of studies—at places like the University of Pittsburgh, the University of Chicago, and Duke University—have shown this. Good nutrition, exercise, and praying with a community all have measurable positive effects on how long we are likely to live.

Part of the reason, I gather, is that in a community, people keep track of each other. If someone is missing from *shul* on Shabbat or church on Sunday, his or her friends wonder what's wrong and they will check up on them. It's the love of one member of the community for another, as Sholom Dovid Winograd might say.

❧ THE JEWISH PRAYER BOOK ❧

The Jewish prayer book, the *Siddur*, is an ancient text that has been in a continual process of being written and edited for more than two thousand years, which helps explain why the services are so long. According to the great medieval sage Maimonides, daily prayer is one of the 613 commandments given by God to the Jewish people in the Torah. Prayer is one of the most significant ways we share in intimacy with God. Originally, prayer could take any form the worshiper liked. In ancient times, it was entirely spontaneous, mixing elements of praise for God, beseeching Him for His gifts and favor, and offering thanks for His loving-kindness.

But over periods of long exile, beginning with the exile to Babylonia, Jews began to lose their fluency with prayer, especially with Hebrew prayer. So the great sages who lived at that time established a basic fixed prayer, the *Amidah*, or Standing Prayer, which was said three times every day—morning, afternoon, and evening—the first two mirroring the sacrifices that had been brought each day at similar times in the Jerusalem Temple.

On the Sabbath, as on other holy days, there is an additional, or *Mussaf*, service after the morning prayer, just as there was an additional sacrifice in the Temple.

Because the prayer book is thick, it can be intimidating. Many regular synagogue goers feel obligated to say every word of every prayer, but I take encouragement from the rabbis of old who counseled, "One may do much, or one may do little, provided he directs his heart to Heaven." It is more important to understand and mean every word of prayer you say than to rush to say every word in the book without understanding its meaning or feeling its spirit. I once heard a contemporary rabbi advise his congregation that if you don't understand Hebrew well, it is better to pray in English. "God," the rabbi said, "will understand your prayers no matter what language they come in."

❧ THE *NESHAMA* PRAYER ☙

Of all the words in the Jewish prayer book, among the most meaningful to me and, I suspect, many others are the words of the prayer called *Modeh Ani*, which I described to you earlier. This is the short prayer we say at home when we wake up.

Another beautiful prayer we say in the synagogue at the very beginning of the morning service on Sabbath and every day strikes the same note as the *Modeh Ani*. This prayer, the *Neshama* or "soul" prayer, affirms that God is not only the Creator of the world and the human race, but also gives each person life by breathing a soul into each one of us. These words of prayer are taken directly from the Bible in Genesis (2:7): "And the Lord God formed man of the dust of the ground, and breathed into his nostrils the breath of life; and man became a living soul."

That's why we speak of the soul as "breath." In Hebrew, that's what the word *neshama* literally means. The breath of life is wrapped up with our soul, as the *Neshama* prayer makes clear.

My God,
the soul You placed within me is pure.
You created it, You formed it, You breathed it into me,

and You guard it while it is within me.
One day You will take it from me,
and restore it to me in the time to come.
As long as the soul is within me,
I will thank You,
Lord my God and the God of my ancestors,
Master of all works, Lord of all souls.
Blessed are You, Lord,
Who restores souls to lifeless bodies.

I have thought about both the *Modeh Ani* and *Neshama* prayers a lot. For me, they contain fundamental truths about the divine origins we each have, about the free will each of our "pure" souls is given, and about the promise of eternal life, as the *Neshama* prayer says, "in the time to come."

The *Neshama* prayer is a perfect example of a prayer I read slowly and often in English because it says so much to me. I don't ever want to rush through it. In fact, when somebody asked me a while ago what was the most memorable spiritual moment of my life, I thought of this prayer and the times I have seen the first breath enter a baby's body and the last leave an adult's. Those have been the most spiritual moments of my life

The first was the birth of our younger daughter, Hani, and the other was the death of my mother, Marcia.

Hani was born at Yale New Haven hospital in March of 1988. It was the first time I was allowed to stay in the delivery room to watch one of my children being born. We arrived at the hospital with Hadassah in labor but otherwise feeling okay. I remember the nurse saying to us, "I'm so glad to see you come in. You look in normal condition. I've had nothing but emergencies all night."

She then put a fetal monitor over Hadassah's abdomen and, when she couldn't find a fetal heartbeat, immediately went into emergency mode. She slammed a button that set off an alarm, and yelled, "Code blue!"

Our baby's umbilical cord was wrapped around her neck—needless to say, a serious complication if not addressed immediately. And just moments before, the nurse said she was glad to see us because we weren't presenting her with an emergency!

The doctors and a lot of pushing by Hadassah (and, of course, a lot of help from God) quickly induced delivery. Suddenly, miraculously, there was a baby. I remember thinking, *A whole, beautiful baby. What a miracle.* As she took her first breath and cried her first big cry, I thought of the *Neshama* prayer and felt that I had witnessed God blowing "the breath of life" into Hani's nostrils.

Seventeen years later, I saw the breath of life leave my ninety-year-old mother's body.

It was June of 2005. Mom had been struggling for almost six months with a cancer of the blood called myelodisplasia. It was clear that her life on earth was coming to an end. Hani was about to leave for summer camp where she was going to be a counselor. She knew that Baba, with whom she was very close, would probably not be alive when she returned, so she came with us to the hospital to say goodbye. We all had a good conversation, and when it was time to leave, Hani went over to kiss her Baba and began to cry. My mother, who had been very weak earlier in the day, sat straight up in her chair and said, "Oh Hani, sweetheart, I know why you're crying.

But please don't cry. I have learned that everything in life has a beginning and an end, including life. I've had a wonderful life. I've been blessed with wonderful family and friends. So, Hani, don't cry."

My mom rose so beautifully to this moment, and she seemed to strengthen and inspire Hani who surprised us all by saying: "I'd like to be alone with Baba." The rest of us left the hospital room. For fifteen minutes they talked alone. I suspect my mother—like a biblical matriarch—gave Hani some missions to carry on in her life. But I do not know exactly what they spoke about. That is a confidence that remains with Hani.

During the next week, my mother's condition became more serious and painful. Before this, pain was something she usually dismissed with a laugh. She had arthritis so bad over the latter part of her life that it hurt even to put on her socks in the morning, but she usually just laughed about it. She was by nature upbeat. But not now.

"Joseph," she said to me on Friday, June 24, "for the first time, I am praying to God to take my *neshama* [my soul] from my body."

Later that Friday, before Shabbat began, Mom fell into a coma.

Two days later, on Sunday night, June 26, God answered her prayer. It was the first time I had seen anyone die. In this case, the death was peaceful for Mom and meaningful for me and the rest of the family gathered around her in our home in Stamford.

We watched her breathe, in and out, in and out. Now more slowly, she took a deep breath, and exhaled. Then she took another deep breath. And she exhaled again. And then her breathing stopped, quietly and peacefully. It was as if I could see the breath of life, the *neshama*, leaving her body.

The special liturgy of the Sabbath is, as I've mentioned, tied closely to the three themes of the day (creation, revelation, and redemption). The first theme, the Creation, began when God breathed life into Adam and is continued every time another baby begins life. Every time I read the *Neshama* prayer in the Sabbath morning service, I grow in my understanding and appreciation that all life comes from God.

❧ SIMPLE BEGINNINGS ❧

- If you are married, and especially if you have small children who tend to burn through a parent's energy, don't forget to make time for romance and intimacy with your spouse on your Sabbath. Dress up. Relax. You don't have to leave your home to have a date night!

- When you wake up the next morning, as soon as you open your eyes and before getting out of bed, thank God for the gift of life that He has given you.

- On your Sabbath, if you like coffee, enjoy it at home with your loved ones in the morning rather than grabbing a commercial cup on your way out to do errands. It doesn't have to be coffee, of course, but think about incorporating simple, enjoyable rituals in your rest day to evoke the unique and restful atmosphere of a Sabbath.

- Consider not wearing a watch on the Sabbath. Don't worry about being late. Your main responsibility today is to rest and, thereby, to please and honor God—not to be on time and please other human beings.

Chapter Five

MORNING PRAYERS:

THE COVENANT OF DESTINY

Saturday Morning Prayers

I know that many of you reading this book are not familiar with the traditions and rituals of Jewish prayer services. So when I recently came across a visitor's account of his experience with Jewish worship, I thought it might be helpful to retell it here as part of our shared experience of the Sabbath.

❧ A NINETEENTH-CENTURY OBSERVATION ❧

More than a century ago, a young Frenchman named Aimé Pallière, who was preparing to be a Roman Catholic priest, visited a synagogue in his hometown of Lyon. He had no experience at all with Judaism. Pallière later wrote a beautifully sympathetic and illuminating book about his exploration of Jewish ideas, *The Unknown Sanctuary*.

It was in 1892, at age seventeen, that he and a friend walked into a synagogue on the Quai Tilsitt in Lyon. The day was actually Yom Kippur, not Shabbat, but the sight they saw would be almost exactly the same on the Sabbath in any synagogue in the world today. The congregation was standing, facing east toward Jerusalem. Every man was wearing a prayer shawl—white with black stripes in a pattern dictated by mystical theology—extending down his back and around his shoulders and trailing tassels, or *tzitzit*, whose distinctive arrangement of knots recalls the number 613, the traditional count of the commandments in the Torah. Pallière recorded very interesting observations in his book.

First, he concluded, it wasn't the Jewish *religion* he encountered as much as the living Jewish *people*. What he knew of the Jews before this was pretty much limited to what he saw in the Doré Bible, with its classic engraved illustrations. This people had been an antiquated abstraction for him, but were now revealed as a combination of the contemporary and the timeless. The rabbis call this the *Knesset Yisrael*, the Congregation of Israel, a collective entity—partially real and partially virtual—which includes all the Jews who ever lived and ever will live, everywhere in the world—a vast and diverse family in a particular relationship with God.

Second, Pallière noticed that everyone appeared to be officiating in the role of *priest*. There was surely a rabbi somewhere around and a prayer leader. But every man in the synagogue was dressed in a prayer shawl and was praying out loud, giving the powerful impression of "collective priesthood."

Finally, the young Frenchman noticed a quality of *waiting*

for or *expecting* something. "It seemed to me that this assembly was in expectancy of something about to happen. What are they waiting for, I asked my companion." The friend had no idea either. Pallière later concluded that the people in the congregation were awaiting nothing less than the Messianic redemption, the "fixing of the world" or *tikkun olam*, the promise that suffuses the Hebrew Bible. We'll return to this theme in a little while.

I wanted to share Pallière's observations because they surprised me and reminded me that the tour I am giving you is influenced by my own limited experience, vision, and thoughts. You will probably have your own reactions as we go through the Sabbath day, and that, I think, is a very good thing.

At the end of the last chapter, we had just finished the preliminary part of the Saturday morning service including the *Neshama* or "soul" prayer. The next part, the *Shaharit* service, was about to begin. At this point, the mood and pace of the service changes. Up until now, the prayers have been personal. Everyone has been quietly, but audibly, reading the psalms of the preliminary part of the service creating the sound of a communal hum. Sometimes it becomes a hubbub when one or another of the congregants spontaneously speaks one of the lines from the psalms quite loudly.

❧ A CLARION CALL TO PRAYER ❧

This ends with a clarion call to prayer from the cantor on the altar. It is called *Borchu*, which means "bless," and is inspired by a passage from the book of Nehemiah:

Then upon the stairs of the Levites [they] stood; . . .
and they cried in a loud voice to the Lord their God.
Then the Levites . . . said, Rise up and bless the Lord
your God from everlasting to everlasting, and let
them bless Thy glorious name. (9:4–5)

Today, in our synagogue, the cantor or lay leader bows and summons us to prayer with the similar words of *Borchu*: "Bless the Lord, the blessed One, forever and all time." To which we all respond, also bowing as we do: "Bless the Lord, the blessed One, forever and all time."

This is one of several times you will see bowing in the synagogue on Shabbat. There is no kneeling or genuflection, but it was not always that way. In the Jerusalem Temple, worshipers performed prostrations, casting their whole body upon the floor as a sign of submission to God. After the Temple was destroyed, the rabbis limited this practice to several times during the prayer services of Rosh Hashanah and Yom Kippur, the New Year and the Day of Atonement, because of the atmosphere of heightened awe that goes with those days. Apparently, the rabbis did not want prostration or kneeling to occur as frequently in the post-Temple synagogues as in the Jerusalem Temple, perhaps intending through this deprivation to whet our appetite and longing to see the Temple rebuilt. Therefore, at this call to prayer, as at other moments in the Shabbat liturgy, we simply bend the knee for a moment and incline the body forward.

The traditional Jewish Sabbath is not like the Sabbath of the early New England Puritans, who spent the whole day in prayer. But prayer is central to the Jewish Sabbath experience.

After the call to prayer, the service has a simple structure that leads to the two central prayers of Jewish daily liturgy, the *Shema* and the *Amidah* which we discussed at the Friday night service. Now let me tell you a little more about each and some thoughts they evoke in me.

❧ THE *SHEMA* ❧

The *Shema*, which means "Hear," is not a typical prayer of petition or expression of gratitude, but a recitation of readings from the Torah that constitute a clear and strong declaration of monotheistic faith. The *Shema* prayer begins with the declaration "Hear, O Israel: The Lord our God; the Lord is One" (Deuteronomy 6:4), followed by three sections of scripture.

The *Shema* is one of the earliest religious thoughts taught to Jewish children and one of the last said by Jewish adults before death. It is one of the oldest Jewish prayers, going back to the time of the Temple in Jerusalem.

The next sections of the *Shema* prayer are from Deuteronomy (6:5–9 and 11:13–21). We are taught there that our goal in life must be to love God, to serve Him with all our heart and all our soul, and to teach God's commandments to our children.

For me, it has always been significant and moving that the *Shema,* which is said every day in synagogues throughout the world, is the same prayer that was said by Jesus in Israel two millennia ago:

And one of the scribes came, and having heard them reasoning together, and perceiving that he had answered them well, asked him, Which is the first commandment of all? And Jesus answered him, The first of all the commandments is, Hear, O Israel; The Lord our God is one Lord: And thou shalt love the Lord thy God with all thy heart, and all thy soul, and with all thy mind, and with all thy strength: this is the first commandment. (Mark 12:28–30 KJV)

Those words from the New Testament are one of many reasons I once began my remarks to a gathering in Washington of Christians United for Israel, an organization founded by my friend, Pastor John Hagee, with five familiar words from Genesis: "I am your brother, Joseph" (Genesis 45:4).

In the final section of the *Shema* (Numbers 15:37–41), we are cautioned not to follow our hearts and eyes, which will naturally lead us astray, but to "be holy to your God—who brought you out of the land of Egypt to be your God."

The Hebrew word *shema* is translated as "hear" in most Jewish prayer books and in the Bible version I have used in most of this book. But in the translation of the Koren Siddur (Prayer Book) I have used—which is by Britain's chief rabbi, Sir Jonathan Sacks—*shema* is rendered "listen." His explanation for this choice is instructive:

I have translated it here as "Listen" rather than the traditional "Hear" because listening is active, hearing is passive. The *Shema* is a call to an act of mind and soul, to meditate on, internalize, and affirm the oneness of God.

Most civilizations have been cultures of the eye. Judaism, with its belief in the invisible God who transcends the universe, is supremely a civilization of the ear.

The words of the *Shema* also remind us of the risks involved in being distracted or corrupted by visual images. As it says in the last section: "Remember all of the Lord's commandments and keep them, not straying after your heart and after your eyes, following your own sinful desires" (Numbers 15:39). There's an important Sabbath lesson here, because the Sabbath is a day when we have the opportunity to listen to people in a way we don't during the rest of the week. Our modern secular culture is very visual, often in unhealthy ways. Our eyes are constantly on televisions, video games, computers, email, websites, and all the rest. Many modern workers spend entire days interacting with a screen. Even if the images we see are all wholesome—and of course they aren't—it is still socially isolating to have such an exclusive relationship with a video screen. It separates us from the company of other people and from civil interaction and social conversation.

The Sabbath forces us to pull our eyes away from the digital flow and rejoin the natural world, where communication is accomplished mainly through human voices speaking and human ears listening. The genius of the Sabbath lies in the way it restricts us from certain activities and, thereby, frees us to experience others including conversations—big ones with God and less grand ones with our family and friends.

The early rabbis were so convinced of the importance of *talking*, *listening*, and *responding* that for centuries they compelled teachers and students to carry on their learning orally. They actually forbade rabbinic opinions and dialogues from being compiled in books, creating the Jewish oral tradition that explains and implements the Bible. But when Jews found themselves exiled from Israel and scattered throughout the Diaspora (the global dispersion of the Jews from Israel), they gradually forgot the traditions of their ancestors. That's when the rabbis permitted the oral teachings to be written down into what are now known as the Mishnah, Talmud, and Midrash.

On the Sabbath, we recapture the culture of speech. Of course, we may read, and I do. Yet even better than reading, which itself can be isolating, is discussion with other people. This emphasis on speech as contrasted with sight is symbolized, as you will see during our congregation's recitation of the *Shema* prayer, by everyone putting their hand over their eyes as they recite the affirmation of faith.

It is particularly important to speak with our children on Shabbat, as the *Shema* also teaches:

> These words which I command you today shall be on your heart. Teach them repeatedly to your children, speaking of them when you sit at home and when you travel on the way, when you lie down and when you rise. (Deuteronomy 6:6–7)

Notice again the emphasis on teaching by *speaking* and on seizing every opportunity that may arise, whether you are at home or out in the world, to talk with your children about loving God and living by His Law. For example, when we're in a car with our children, we are naturally tempted to listen to music or the news. Since the Sabbath prohibits us from driving and from using electronic sound, we must walk; and when we walk, we end up talking with our children.

Chief Rabbi Sacks has a wonderfully relevant interpretation of the directive in the *Shema* to "teach them [the values and commandments of the Torah] repeatedly to your children." He writes:

> Education is the responsibility, not only of schools, but also of parents. In Judaism, parents are educators, the home a matrix of learning, and education a conversation across the generations. Alshich [a sixteenth-century rabbinic sage who lived in Safed, Israel] connects this verse to the earlier one ("Love God"): How do we teach our children? By showing them what we love.

So talk to your children, as early as they will listen, about loving God and about how He made the world and everything in it.

My granddaughter, Maddy, was apparently taught these lessons well by her parents, Becca and Jacob. Once during a bath when she was two, her mom told her that she had a very cute "tush" and Maddy responded, "That's because God made my tush."

I am very grateful to my four children for the way they have listened and learned and live. Each of them has brought Shabbat into their lives, and now into the lives of their children. All of them are building strong links in the chain of Jewish history and destiny that I worried would be broken when my grandmother, Baba, passed away.

This brings to mind a special interpretation of the *Shema* that I once heard in a sermon. In the Bible, our forefather, Jacob, is also called Israel. So, the rabbi said, when we read, "Hear, O Israel, the Lord is our God, the Lord is One," we can hear "Israel" as a reference not to the nation but to our forefather Jacob. We can imagine that those are the words Jacob's sons said to him, Israel, at the end of his life, assuring him that they, too, believed in and loved God, as he did, and would continue to love and serve Him. We can be certain that made Jacob feel very good. Each time we say the *Shema* today, the rabbi concluded, we are giving the same assurance to our parents and theirs, all the way back to Israel, Isaac, and Abraham. That is certainly the comforting message I receive each time I hear my children or grandchildren saying the *Shema* or see them living lives that express how much they embrace the *Shema*'s call to love and serve God.

Although the *Shema* prayer doesn't use the word "destiny," which I will focus on next in explaining the *Amidah* prayer, it does explicitly embrace the promise that God gave to Abraham, Isaac, and Jacob that the destiny of their children was to be in the land of Israel. In the prayers immediately before the *Shema* declaration we say: "May you make a new light shine over Zion, and may we all soon be worthy of its light." And "Bring us back in peace from the four quarters of the earth and lead us upright to our land."

Then in the second paragraph of the *Shema* is the promise that the ultimate result of loving and serving God will be "that you and your children may live long in the land that the Lord swore to your ancestors to give them, for as long as the heavens are above the earth."

❧ THE *AMIDAH* ☙

After the *Shema* and a few transitional prayers, the Sabbath morning service builds to one of its climactic moments. It is time for the *Amidah*. The congregation rises and stands as erect as possible, inspired by that vision from Ezekiel 1:7 of the angels of God standing straight up. Before beginning the silent prayer we take three steps back and then three steps forward to remind ourselves that we are approaching the King of Kings. We are entering a holy space. Our speech is silent and direct, following the example of Hannah as she prayed to be able to have a child in 1 Samuel 1:13: "Now Hannah spoke in her heart: only her lips moved, but her voice was not heard."

As you may recall, the *Amidah*—which is said at every Jewish service—contains three parts: praise, petition, and gratitude. As I explained in chapter 2, the focus of the *Amidah* on Shabbat morning is God's revelation in history when He gave us the Ten Commandments and the Torah. Most of the middle part of the morning *Amidah* is a recitation of excerpts from Exodus about the revelation at Sinai and the receiving of the commandments, focusing on the commandment to observe the Sabbath.

I want to discuss with you one key phrase in the Shabbat morning *Amidah*, because I think it will help you better understand the Sabbath and the view of life that emerges from it. The first sentence in the first paragraph of the middle section of this morning's *Amidah* is generally translated as:

Moses rejoiced at the gift of his portion
when You called him "faithful servant" . . .

He brought down in his hands two tablets of stone
on which was engraved the observance of the Sabbath.

But Rabbi David de Sola Pool's prayer book gives a different, creative, and—I think—very meaningful translation of a few of those words. Instead of saying Moses rejoiced in "the gift of his portion," Rabbi de Sola Pool says, Moses rejoiced at "the *destiny* bestowed on him."

This is important to me, because I believe the word *destiny* is at the heart of the Jewish religious experience.

❧ LIVING OUT OUR DESTINY ❧

As the Shabbat morning *Amidah* reminds us of God's revelation at Mt. Sinai, it also challenges us to consider the choices we make regarding whether or not to live out God's destiny for our lives. When Moses brought down the tablets from the mountain, he brought not just the Commandments, "the gift of his portion," but human *destiny*. God's revelation of Himself was His way of telling us He continued to care about His creation (which is commemorated in the Friday night service) and how we behave. For us, it is also God's road map to what we can be—what we are *destined* to be, individually and collectively—if we follow that road map. Collectively, depending on your faith and beliefs, it can lead to the age of the Messiah and eternal life. Individually, it can lead us to live better lives by inspiring us to actualize all the potential we have been given.

Do I believe that God has a plan for each of us? Well, I certainly believe that the values given at Sinai are a plan each of us is called on to follow. And I believe that God did not just create the world and go away. I believe that He continues to act in the world and that we each have the capacity to be His partners in action if we choose His commandments and values as our destiny. At different times in my life, I have been inspired, motivated, or strengthened by that belief and by the belief others have had in my destiny.

This began before I was even born. My grandmother, Baba, emigrated to America from Europe, from an area in the Carpathian mountains in what is now Ukraine. The righteous rabbi who led the Orthodox Hasidic sect that Baba was a part of also emigrated to New York and came to Connecticut once a year to see my Baba and other followers there. His last name was Horowitz. On one such visit, he asked my mother, who had then been married three years, why she did not have a baby yet. "She is having trouble getting pregnant," Baba said to him in Yiddish.

Rabbi Horowitz then gave my mother a blessing and said, "You will soon become pregnant and give birth to a son who will be a leader of the people." That, in case you were wondering, turned out to be me.

I heard this story (from my thoroughly unbiased mother and father) during my childhood; I have sometimes wondered what effect it had on me and my career choice. But I hasten to add that I am not saying that God elected me to be a leader. I have always loved Lincoln's reply to a group of ministers who visited the White House to tell him that they were sure God was on the side of the North in the Civil War. Lincoln responded that one cannot know God's mind definitively so we cannot be sure that God is on our side. But we can and must work hard to be on God's side.

In 1980, after serving ten years in the Connecticut state senate, I ran for Congress and lost and then had another brush with the idea of destiny. The morning after election day, I received a call from Father Joseph Dilion, the pastor of St. Brendan's Catholic Church in the neighborhood where I lived in New Haven. Father Dilion and I became good friends during the years I had been his state senator and he had been, as I called him, "my parish priest." He called me the morning after that election loss in 1980 and said, "Joe, I know you must be feeling shaken this morning. But please believe me, God is saving you for something better."

I cannot express how much those words meant to me that morning. Two years later when I was elected attorney general of Connecticut, Father Dilion called the morning after to congratulate me and tell me he hoped I never doubted his faith in my . . . well, destiny. And six years after that, when I was elected to the U.S. Senate, the good Father called again and this time we just laughed a lot and agreed that God is very good!

I was raised with two pieces of rabbinical wisdom that seem relevant here. The first is that when I get to the gates of heaven, I will not be asked whether during my life I had been as good as Moses, but whether I had been as good as Joe Lieberman could have been. The second is from the Mishnah's tractate Ethics of the Fathers. Rabbi Tarfon taught, "The day is short, the task is great, the laborers are lazy, the reward is much, and the Master is insistent." However, he also said, "It is not for you to complete the task, but neither are you free to stand aside from it."

❧ An Unexpected Conversation ❦

I want to share an unexpected experience I had during 2008 (although some might say it was "destined" to happen) about the concept of "destiny."

It was a Sunday afternoon in September at the Westin Hotel in downtown Philadelphia where Governor Sarah Palin was preparing for her vice presidential debate which would occur on the following Thursday—a difficult time for her in the 2008 national campaign. I was asked to be there to help with the preparation because I had endorsed my friend John McCain for president and had some vice presidential debate experience myself. I had met Sarah Palin at the Republican Convention in Minneapolis and was impressed by her strong and effective acceptance speech.

When I arrived at the debate prep, which was being held in a crowded hotel suite, some of the McCain staff were asking the governor potential debate questions. I saw a very different Sarah Palin than I had seen in Minneapolis. She seemed tired and distracted. Her answers were halting or confused. The first part of her embarrassing interview with Katie Couric had just aired, and I wondered whether her confidence was broken. Several of McCain's team members and campaign leadership were in that crowded suite, including the managers, Rick Davis and Steve Schmidt, and they were visibly nervous. One of them called a break, and most of us left the room except for the governor and her friend and former chief of staff from Alaska, Kris Perry. Out in the hall, the McCain campaign was in a panic over Palin's performance. They understood that she was tired from intensive campaigning. Someone said she probably missed her infant child, Trig.

There was talk about flying her out to the McCain family ranch in Arizona for the rest of her debate preparation and bringing her husband and the baby to be there with her.

In the midst of this "what are we going to do now" moment, Steve Schmidt turned to me and said, "Senator, you have something in common with her that none of the rest of us has. You're both religious. Please go in there and talk to her and maybe pray with her."

This was a wonderfully Judeo-Christian sentiment, because although Sarah Palin is clearly Christian and I am clearly Jewish, Schmidt understood that there might be a special bond between us based on our religious beliefs and observance. He was right. I have often experienced this interreligious connection among believers throughout my life. It transcends faiths and denominations.

I wanted to help the McCain campaign and therefore Palin; but praying with a person I hardly knew seemed artificial. So I went into the debate prep room where Governor Palin was sitting with Kris Perry and just asked, "How are you doing?"

"Okay." she said. "But I haven't been at my best today."

Palin felt badly treated by some members of the McCain campaign staff, and she knew they were worried about her performance as a candidate.

"Governor," I said, "you and I are both people of faith. We believe most things happen for a reason. You *must* be here for a reason."

She laughed and said that was exactly what she had been thinking. "How else," she said, "can I explain why and how I am here as the candidate for vice president of the United States?"

I asked her if she knew the biblical story of Queen Esther, the young Jewish woman who became Queen of Persia at the very time that the king's evil minister, Haman, was plotting the destruction of the Jewish people. As I expected, she said she knew the story well and loved it.

When Queen Esther learned of the plot, she at first despaired and was afraid to approach the king for help. She felt powerless to save her people. Then her uncle, Mordechai, told her she must consider her *destiny*. "Who knows whether thou art not come to royal estate for such a time as this?" (Esther 4:14). Esther shook off her doubts and took action, courageously confronting Haman and successfully convincing the king to save her people. She made a choice and realized her destiny.

"You are at a moment of personal destiny," I said to Palin. "You have been given a big opportunity, and you have a choice to make about whether or not you will seize it and your destiny. So be yourself and have faith, and God will see you through this."

"Those words mean a lot to me right now," Sarah said.

"I'm glad to hear that," I responded. "If you have a couple of minutes, I have another thought that just came to mind."

"Stay as long as you can," her aide Kris said. "This is the best conversation we've had all day."

I had just been reading a beautiful essay by Rabbi Soloveitchik, called *Kol Dodi Dofek*. The title of the essay is a phrase from the biblical Song of Songs in Hebrew, which means, "Listen—My Beloved Knocks." In the Song of Songs, as we have discussed, when God knocks on His beloved's door, she is lazy and self-involved and puts off opening the door. When she finally does, He is gone, leaving them both brokenhearted. Rabbi Soloveitchik makes the point in *Kol Dodi Dofek* that there are times in the life of every person—and of every community and nation—when the knock comes at our door, when opportunity, or destiny, comes within our reach, and we are challenged to answer it before the opportunity passes and our destiny slips away.

Rabbi Soloveitchik goes on to offer a profound insight—which I shared with Governor Palin that day—that there are different covenants that God has entered into with us. The first is the Covenant of Fate, which does not require our active participation. God chose the Children of Israel on the basis of their being descendants of the patriarch Abraham, whose heart, in the words of the liturgy, God found to be "steadfast." Abraham's descendants were in a covenantal relationship with God as a matter of fate. That is the Covenant of Fate.

But there is also the Covenant of Destiny, which is very different. When the children of Israel stood at the foot of Mt. Sinai, they actively signaled their agreement to join themselves to God by accepting the Ten Commandments and the Torah: "All that the Lord has said will we do, and obey," they proclaimed (Exodus 24:7). They were accepting their destiny. Destiny, unlike fate, involves choice. God may have a destiny in mind for each of us, but He leaves it up to us to decide if we will answer His knock at our door. The Covenant of Fate is what we are. The Covenant of Destiny is what we can make of ourselves.

I did my best to communicate that concept to Sarah Palin in my conversation with her that Sunday afternoon. "This is your moment," I said to her. "Use all the ability you have to take advantage of this opportunity to realize your destiny."

And I believe she did.

•   •   •

The revelation at Sinai, which is our focus in the Sabbath morning service, is about destiny. It is not about what we are. It is about what we are destined to become and how following the commandments Moses received from God on Sinai can help us become that. By telling us how to live, the commandments give us our mission—if we choose to accept it—of bettering, even perfecting, the world God created. The two Hebrew words, *tikkun olam*—which mean to "perfect the world"—have come to summarize life's goals for many Jews. The idea appears in a prayer called *Aleynu,* said at the end of all Jewish services, in a sentence that means "when the world will be perfected under the sovereignty of the Almighty." That is our destiny as individuals and as a civilization. I was taught that the Children of Israel became a nation, not when they were liberated from slavery, but when the Law was revealed to them on Sinai—because that gave them their reason for being, their national destiny. Those same values give each of us a personal destiny. But you can't be passive about your destiny. It isn't fulfilled unless you decide to work to make it happen.

The commandment to observe the Sabbath is part of the revelation and therefore, to me, is at the heart of our destiny. But the Sabbath also doesn't automatically enter our lives. We have to decide to bring it in, to seize that part of our destiny. And that can be difficult.

When it comes to accepting the gift of rest that God offers us all, we need to strengthen ourselves to overcome the natural forces of resistance in our competitive society. They may come from social pressure not to be "different," or from other people who want us to go to the movies or shopping with them on the Sabbath, or from colleagues who are at work on the Sabbath. It takes an independence of spirit, one that needs to be deliberately developed, to defy the pressure to conform.

My religious observance, including my Sabbath observance, has taught me that it's okay to be different, and I think that has made it easier for me to be different in my political life when being different is where my beliefs have taken me. When you choose your own path—whether in faith, politics, or whatever you do—you will not only feel better, but other people will generally respect you for your choice. And if they don't, well, that's their right, just as it is yours to do what you believe is your right and your destiny.

Now we return to the synagogue where the congregation has finished its silent *Amidah* prayer and the cantor or lay leader sings a very special section called the *Kedushah* (Holiness).

In the *Kedushah*, we sing the words of praise to God from Isaiah's vision, as spoken by the angels. These familiar words are heard in the Catholic mass and many Protestant church services.

> *Holy, holy, holy, is the Lord of hosts:*
> *the whole earth is full of His glory. (6:3)*

Still standing as tall as each of us can, with our feet together, we rise to our toes each time we say the word "Holy," as if we are reaching to join the heavenly angels. The central kabbalistic text, the *Zohar*, speaks of the words, "The whole world is full of God's glory" in a way that relates directly back to our discussion of destiny. The *Zohar* says those words teach us that people have the miraculous power to become like angels and bring God's holiness to earth, if only we love and serve God. And that is how the whole world can be truly full of God's glory.

The *Kedushah* also prepares us for the reenactment of the Sinai revelation, when we publicly read the Torah on Saturday morning. From the transcendent high of adoring God in the company of the angels, we move to encounter Him more concretely in the words of the Bible.

The Sinai moment in the Sabbath morning service—when God's message to us is revealed—has come.

❧ SIMPLE BEGINNINGS ❧

❧ If you attend worship services at a church or synagogue on the Sabbath or Sunday morning, consider choosing a congregation close enough that you can walk there and home again. Liberate yourself from the automobile! If you do drive, leave the radio off. Enjoy this quiet time to think or talk with your family.

❧ If you don't belong to a church or synagogue, look for one where you feel comfortable and happy. Listen to your heart. Authenticity comes through and can be recognizable even before we are theologically or philosophically connected. Pray by yourself whenever you can, but also seek opportunities to pray with a community.

❧ Use the occasion of your Sabbath day to study God's word on your own and to talk about it. In fact, even if you're not discussing the Bible or other holy works, go out of your way on this day of rest to interact personally with other people. The Sabbath isn't a time to hole up in your house and meditate in silence. It's a day to interact with God's creations.

❧ Consider the question: What is my destiny? What special plan does God have for me, what mission in life, that He is holding out to me and inviting me to pursue?

☙ Chapter Six ❧

THE TORAH READING:

REVERING GOD'S WORD

———————

Saturday Morning

W hen the time comes for the public reading of the Torah on Sabbath morning, the service becomes its most grandly ceremonial. During this part of the morning service, several congregants are called up to participate, and that is a great honor.

☙ PRESENTING THE TORAH ❧

As we prepare for the reading, the congregation stands and three of its members come to the front of the sanctuary. The first opens the curtains and doors of the Ark, a chamber in the eastern front wall that contains the Torah. The second removes the Torah from the Ark. This Torah is not a printed book. It is, as it has been since ancient times, a scroll of special parchment on which the words of the Five Books of Moses are written in special ink by a specially trained scribe. The parchment is about three feet in height and wound thickly around two poles, all of which are covered in embroidered velvet and adorned, like a king, with a silver crown. When the Ark is opened, the congregation first sings the words from Numbers that Moses spoke when the Ark of the Covenant traveled in the desert:

> Whenever the Ark set out, Moses would say,
> "Arise, Lord, and may Your enemies be scattered.
> May those who hate You flee before You." (10:35)

That is followed by the words of Isaiah in a triumphal song:

> For the Torah shall come forth from Zion, and the word of
> the Lord from Jerusalem. (2:3)

With the Ark still open, the person holding the Torah hands it to the third person who turns to the congregation; together we recite a beautiful prayer taken from the text of the *Zohar*, the ancient Jewish work of mystical explanations of the Torah. Known by its first two words, *B'reech Sh'may* ("Blessed is the Name"), this prayer is premised on the kabbalistic belief that when the Ark is opened and the Torah removed for public reading, the gates of heaven also open, and God's love and compassion are stirred by our continuing commitment to read and hear His word. The prayer itself is as personal and passionate as the Kabbalists were.

The person who is holding the Torah then sings the words of the *Shema*, "Listen, O Israel, the Lord our God, the Lord is One," and the congregation repeats that great monotheistic declaration aloud in song. So, in these few prayers before the Torah is opened and read, we have gone right back to the fundamentals of our faith, publicly affirming our belief in One God and in the divinely inspired truth of His Scriptures.

Now the Ark is closed, and the person holding the Torah carries it through the congregation. The members reach out to kiss its cover or to touch their prayer books or the fringes of their prayer shawls to the passing Torah and then to their lips.

I have witnessed this ceremony so many times that I have begun to take its grandeur for granted. It is, in fact, magnificent and moving. The ceremony of the Torah being held up and carried through the adoring congregation may remind you of times you have seen religious statues or icons carried through other adoring congregations of other faiths. That is a relevant and important insight because we believe the words written on this scroll are divinely inspired. And that helps explain why the Jewish people have come to be known as the "People of the Book." As Chief Rabbi Sacks has written,

> Since the revelation at Mt. Sinai, the Jewish people have been defined by a book: The Torah. Just as the Torah is central to Jewish life, so is the reading of the Torah central to the synagogue service.

After the procession is completed, the Torah is set down on a draped reading table, which in some synagogues, like my Georgetown synagogue, is located on the raised altar in front of the sanctuary, near the Ark; and in others, like my Stamford synagogue, further back in the middle of the congregation. The Torah's silver crown and velvet cover are removed, and the scroll is opened to the place where this week's reading is found.

According to Jewish tradition, the practice of publicly reading from the Torah was first decreed by Moses himself. It was reestablished during the Babylonian exile by Ezra the Scribe in the fifth century B.C. and has continued each Saturday since then through the rebuilding of the second Jerusalem Temple, its destruction by the Romans, and the long Diaspora that followed.

The rabbis have divided the Five Books of Moses into weekly portions, so that the entire Torah from Genesis to Deuteronomy—from creation to Moses' death—is sequentially read each year, ending and beginning on the holiday of Simchat Torah, the Celebration of the Torah, which occurs at the end of Sukkot, the Festival of Tabernacles, each fall.

❧ READING THE TORAH ❧

Each weekly reading is divided into seven sections (there's that important and familiar number again). Before each of the seven sections is read, a member of the congregation is called up to bless God: "Bless the Lord, the blessed One." To which the congregation responds, "Bless the Lord, the blessed One, for ever and all time." And then the honoree declares: "Blessed are You, Lord our God, King of the Universe, who has chosen us from all peoples and has given us His Torah. Blessed are You Lord, Giver of the Torah."

The first of the seven people called to the Torah is always a *Kohane*, a descendant of the first high priest, Moses' brother Aaron. Aaron's succeeding generations presided in the Temple in Jerusalem. The second person called is always a descendant of the Levites, who assisted the priests. Although the Temple was destroyed almost two thousand years ago, the descendants of the priests and Levites are given the first honors of the Torah reading out of respect for the lost sanctuary. Lineal descent is what matters; it doesn't matter whether you are one of the wealthiest or most accomplished members of the congregation or one of the poorest or least accomplished. If you are descended from the priests and Levites, you come first and second. Though a U.S. senator, if I am chosen as one of the seven, I come third, at best, because I am neither a descendant of Aaron nor of Levi, but merely one of the Children of Israel.

☙ SEVEN AGAIN ❧

There are two interesting reasons given regarding why the weekly Torah portion is divided into seven shorter readings. The first, as the Talmud teaches, is that seven is the number of advisors that the Jewish kings had (according to Jeremiah 52:25). One function of these advisors was to study and explain the Torah to the king, who was commanded by the Bible to copy for himself the entire Torah scroll and keep it by his side at all times. The important message of this commandment was that the king couldn't make up the law to suit his own views. Everything he did needed to be based on the Torah, God's law, which is always above him. The king must serve God, the true Lawgiver. But the king, like all the rest of us, required help to understand what the Torah really means by its often cryptic statements. So each king appointed seven learned advisors who issued rulings on legal and ethical matters. Seven meant that when they took a vote on a particular question, there would always be a clear result. Rabbi Soloveitchik teaches that the reason we have the same number of congregants called to bless God during the Torah reading as the king had advisors is to remind us to think of the Torah and its rabbinical interpretations as our own personal advisors.

The second and most obvious reason the Torah reading is divided into seven parts is that there are seven days in the week. Some people have the personal custom of reading and studying one of these sections on each day of the week before Saturday, reflecting on what the reading has to say about the particular day in their own life.

A rich tradition of Bible commentary by Jewish scholars over the centuries has now been published in English and is increasingly read and studied by Christians as well as Jews. A while ago, for example, I discovered that my friend and former Senate colleague Sam Brownback of Kansas had been given a copy of the Torah with commentaries, published by the pioneering Jewish publishing company Artscroll. Sam, who is a devout Roman Catholic, was fascinated and enriched by the commentaries from ancient, medieval, and modern sources on the Torah. We have enjoyed discussing their insights.

❦ THE VERY WORDS OF GOD ❦

The parchment on which the Torah is written is, of course, only a medium. The words that are written on it are what matters. Because we believe they are the words of God, when we listen to the Torah chanted aloud in the synagogue or study the words of the Torah before or after the service, we are not just listening to a story and discussing it. We are also coming close to God's truth.

As Maimonides, the twelfth-century Spanish Jewish scholar, wrote in his Principles of Faith:

> I believe with perfect faith that all the words of the prophets are true.
>
> I believe with perfect faith that the prophecy of Moses our teacher, peace be upon him, was true, and that he was the father of the prophets—those who preceded him and those who followed him.
>
> I believe with perfect faith that the entire Torah now in our hands is the same one that was given to Moses, our teacher, peace be upon him.

I quote from these ancient principles of faith to make a point that is at the beating heart of my faith and, I know, the faith of millions and millions of other people—Jews, Christians, and others. We believe in the truth of the Bible, and for us, that truth answers big questions about life and death that we could not otherwise answer.

As an example, let me take the big question of how the Earth and we got here. Was it by accident or design? My observational, deductive answer is encapsulated in the wonderful story of the old rabbi and the young student who were debating the accident/design question about how the Earth with its mantle of life came into being. The rabbi said, "I have an appointment so I must go now, but please come to my house at five this afternoon, and we will continue our discussion."

Promptly at five, the student knocked on the rabbi's door and was welcomed by the rabbi's wife, who asked him to wait in their sitting room. When the student sat down, his eyes were drawn to a large and beautiful landscape painting of mountains, streams, trees, flowers, animals, and people.

The rabbi entered the waiting room and greeted the skeptical student who exclaimed, "Rabbi, I am very impressed by this painting. Who is the artist?"

"Actually," the rabbi said, "there was no artist. A house painter was working here, and his table of paints accidentally fell over, and that painting is the result."

"That's impossible, Rabbi," the student said. "You must be joking."

And, of course, the rabbi said: "You find it impossible to believe that this beautiful painting happened by accident and yet you nevertheless argue that our much more beautiful world was created by accident."

I agree with the rabbi.

When I observe the magnificent order, beauty, and sophistication of the natural and human universe, I simply cannot believe that it all just happened by accident. The words of the Bible that describe God's creation express and, in a real way, validate my belief because I have "perfect faith," as Maimonides put it, that the Bible is the truth.

❧ APPLYING THE TORAH TO LIFE ❧

When the Torah moves around the synagogue, when it "sets out" and "goes forth," its movement symbolizes something important. God's revelation to us has an eternal and unchanging aspect. But it also has a dynamic human side. It's *on the move*. The Torah is literally, as we see in the procession through the synagogue, in our hands, symbolizing, for me, that we are partners with God in implementing the values of the Bible in our lives and through history.

This partnership is seen in our reverence for both God's words and the traditions and teachings that have been passed down from generation to generation. The specific laws of Sabbath observance offer an excellent illustration of the partnership between God and man. When you read the Ten Commandments directly from the Bible, you will have a hard time picturing exactly what the Sabbath of the Fourth Commandment is meant to be. God chose to be sparing in the details but, according to our tradition, He also taught Moses what guarding and remembering the Sabbath means, and the rabbis of the Talmud partnered with God and took it from there. Earlier, we discussed the thirty-nine forms of creative work that the rabbis decided would explain the Torah's prohibition against Sabbath work. But, of course, those categories also had to be defined and explained as laws people could understand, and then they needed to be applied to real situations that come up all the time on the Sabbath. In the Talmud, you'll find the original record of that explaining, formulating, and applying. The process of legal interpretation has been going on for centuries, down to our own day. The work of understanding the Torah and applying it to our lives is never done.

This is true not only of the legal aspects of the Torah, but also of its philosophical and spiritual sides. In his book, *Tanya*, Rabbi Shneur Zalman of Liadi taught that each year at Rosh Hashanah, the Jewish New Year, a new light of understanding bursts forth to us, allowing human beings to illuminate and understand ideas in the Torah that previously had been darkened and concealed. The Torah is eternal and unchanging, yet our understanding of it continually deepens and expands. I can tell you that almost every Shabbat morning I see something in the Torah reading of the week I had not seen or understood before, even though I have been reading the Hebrew Bible over and over for decades.

That is why synagogues are not just houses of prayer, but also houses of *study*. In my two synagogues, there are Torah study groups before and after the Saturday morning and afternoon services. And the rabbi gives a substantial sermon on Saturday morning, after the Torah is read, usually based on the reading for that week, which we will discuss in a little while.

My mother used to tell a story from her childhood that says a lot about Torah study and how much it has advanced in recent times, becoming more accessible to men and women of all backgrounds. Mom remembered seeing her mother, my Baba, sitting in the old synagogue building in Stamford, dressed in her best black dress and black pillbox hat, reading the Torah portion of the week to the women seated around her. She was reading from a Yiddish translation of the Torah, popular with women who didn't understand the Hebrew in which the Torah is chanted. The book was known in Yiddish as the *Tsenerene*, from the Hebrew, *Tze'enah u-Re'enah*, which means "Go forth and gaze." That phrase is from the Song of Songs: "Go forth, O daughters of Zion, and behold King Solomon, with the crown with which his mother crowned him on the day of his wedding, and on the day of the gladness of his heart" (3:11). In the allegorical meaning that Jewish tradition ascribes to the Song of Songs, the verse invites women to gaze not upon Solomon, but upon God Himself on the day when God gave the Ten Commandments and Torah at Mt. Sinai. So in the name of this Yiddish translation of the Bible, a lot was being said about the relationship of love between God and man and the centrality of the Bible in that relationship.

Once, Mom asked her mother why the other women needed her to read the Torah portion to them. Why didn't they have their own copy of the *Tsenerene* so they could read it to themselves?

"Oh," Baba answered, "they always forget their glasses." Years later, Mom realized that Baba was protecting the reputations of the other women. The truth was they were illiterate. They understood Yiddish but could not read it.

For me, this family story is not only a reminder of what a good person my grandmother was but also of how important the study of the Torah has been to Jewish continuity and how much Jewish and Hebraic literacy has expanded in our time. In traditional Jewish communities today, the idea of women unable to read and interpret the Hebrew text itself would be unthinkable.

Years later my mother told this story of her mother's reading the Torah in Yiddish to the other women at a dinner where she was honored by Nishmat, a modern Israeli seminary of Jewish learning for women. She used the story to remind everyone of the responsibility given to parents in the *Shema* prayer to educate our children. Mom also stressed how much better parents are doing today in fulfilling that responsibility for their daughters' education than they did in her mothers' time and hers. In fact, our younger daughter Hani spent a very fruitful year studying at Nishmat.

❧ PRAYER FOR THE SICK ❧

Between sections of the Torah reading many synagogues—including mine—pause for a very personal (yet public) prayer for the recovery of people who are sick. This prayer brings a current and intimate concern into the middle of an ancient and epic reading. The prayer is said in the middle of the Torah reading because we believe that the gates of heaven are open and God's mercy is aroused when His Bible is being read. What better time to pray for family or friends who are sick.

In some synagogues, usually smaller ones, the rabbi or leader reads the prayer aloud; and when it comes time to say the person's name, he looks around the congregation and people call out the names of the ill. Then the rabbi or leader repeats them aloud. In other, larger synagogues, the prayer is read aloud, and the rabbi or leader pauses when it is time for the names of the ill, and each congregant says the name(s) quietly. Incidentally, the names are said in Hebrew, if known, using the mother's name—not the father's, as is otherwise customary—as in Michael, son of Rebecca. Using the mother's name rather than the father's is thought to evoke greater heavenly compassion. The names can be said in English if the Hebrew name of the person who is sick is not known, or if the person being prayed for is not Jewish or doesn't have a Hebrew name.

I believe in prayer. As it says in Psalm 116, "I love the Lord who hears my voice and my supplications. Because he has inclined His ear to me, therefore I will call upon Him as long as I live." So when I hear that people I know or their relatives are sick, I pray for their recovery, on the Sabbath and every day during my morning prayers. I keep a list of names in my mind of those I am praying for. If I run into one of them, I ask how they are doing and tell them I've been praying for them but usually add, "I'm praying for your recovery, Tom, but as much as I believe in prayer, I trust you will not stop going to your doctor."

I have been greatly influenced in these prayers by an insight of Rabbi Soloveitchik who taught that if you know someone who is sick and do not pray for his or her recovery, it is as unacceptable as if you saw that person become ill on the street and did not stop to help him, if only to call a medical professional who could help. That is the spirit in which these public prayers for people who are ill occur on Saturday morning during the Torah reading. When the names are called aloud, this custom also has the practical effect of informing the congregation of who is not feeling well, and one hopes that knowledge will lead members to call or visit that person.

When the Torah reading is completed, two more members of the congregation are called up. One—hopefully in good physical shape—opens the Torah scroll so that at least three columns of writing are visible and then raises the Torah up, above his head if he is able, so the congregation can see the words of the Torah. Everyone then sings:

> *This is the Torah that Moses placed before the Children of Israel, at the Lord's commandment by the hand of Moses.*

Thus, after—as before—the Torah reading, we have declared our faith that the words we have just heard read are the same words God spoke to Moses. The holder of the Torah sits down, usually on a beautiful chair in front of the congregation, and the other person who was called rewinds the scrolls and puts the velvet covering and silver crown back on.

❧ CHANTING THE *HAFTARA* ❧

The last person who is called to say the blessing before the last section of the weekly Torah reading is also honored to chant the *Haftara,* or reading from the Prophets, which follows the Torah reading each week.

A few years ago, while I was in the upstairs main sanctuary of my Stamford synagogue and the congregation was about to hear this reading, I heard a voice behind me say, "Senator, we need you downstairs. There is a medical emergency." I raised my head and saw Irwin Niedober, my friend and fellow congregant, looking serious and whispering gravely. Normally, Irwin is full of cheer. Almost every synagogue I have prayed in has a candy man who has a handy pocketful of candy to distribute to children and interested adults. Irwin is the candy man in Stamford. But now, he seemed very serious, or was he? I looked at him confusedly. If it was a doctor he needed, there were plenty of them in the synagogue.

Then Irwin gave me a meaningful look, and a twinkle entered his eye: "We need you immediately to help administer the medicine." I finally got it. Besides guarding the synagogue's stash of candy, Irwin also had the keys to the liquor cabinet. In a moment, I was on my feet, following him downstairs to the small social hall—to administer the medicine to myself.

In many Orthodox synagogues, as the *Haftara* was being chanted and the words of the Prophets—the great Isaiah or Jeremiah or Ezekiel—filled the sanctuary, a group of congregants quietly (and, some hoped, covertly) left to say an early *Kiddush* usually over a shot of single malt scotch. In many places, these not-so-secret societies came to be known as *Kiddush* clubs.

On this particular occasion in Stamford when Irwin summoned me to a "medical emergency," the rabbi followed the miscreants downstairs, pushed open the door, and chastised us, "This is outrageous! You simply should not be doing this during services and while the *Haftara* is being chanted. It is disrespectful at best."

When he caught sight of me, holding a disposable plastic shot cup full of golden brown scotch, the rabbi left the room.

Later that morning he apologized to me.

"No, Rabbi," I said, "I owe you an apology. You were right."

And of course, he was. There was no excuse. The only explanation I can give is that boys will be boys, even when they are older boys, and in regard to *Kiddush* clubs occasionally girls will be girls, particularly during three-hour-long religious services.

A short while later, the spreading problem of *Kiddush* clubs was unambiguously denounced by the umbrella organization of Orthodox congregations, the Orthodox Union, or OU. It directed its member synagogues to close down the *Kiddush* clubs, like federal agents terminating Prohibition-era speak-easies.

I am pleased to tell you that this dark chapter has now ended in both of the synagogues I regularly attend and in most (but not all) synagogues in America. And that means that we now stay in our seats in the sanctuary as the chanting from the Prophets, the *Haftara*, begins.

The practice of doing a public reading from the Prophets on Saturday morning has both theological and political origins. It began in the second century B.C. when the Syrian-Greek King Antiochus (the king against whom the Maccabees rebelled in the Chanukah story) issued a decree prohibiting public reading from the Torah on the Sabbath, so as to restrict Jewish religious practice and diminish Jewish identity. The leading rabbis of the time satisfied the letter of the royal edict, but not its spirit. In place of the banned Torah reading of the week, they substituted a reading from the Prophets that was reminiscent in theme or content of the Torah reading. After the ban ended and the Torah readings began again, the custom of prophetic readings continued right up to our day. But the particular *Haftara* read each week is still selected because it has some thematic connection to the Torah reading of the week.

The Prophets sing eloquently of the restoration of all the biblical institutions that seem so distant to us now. For example, the *Haftara* we read when the Sabbath falls on the New Moon is from the last chapter of Isaiah. It movingly describes the return of the Israelites to Zion, how the nations of the world will aid and welcome the reestablishment of the Jewish commonwealth in the Holy Land, how God will restore the Temple priesthood, how the Sabbath will be the focal point of a restored universal belief in God: "It shall come to pass, that every new moon, and every Sabbath, shall all flesh come to bow down to the ground before Me, says the Lord" (Isaiah 66:23).

Reading the Prophets reminds us that we are in a transitional time in history. We are on a path to somewhere better. Today is not the day of destiny God envisions for us. But tomorrow holds all the glorious prospect of an even closer relationship between God and man that is centered on the laws and values described in the Bible. That is where the Prophets and history are directing us.

⚜ RETURNING THE TORAH TO THE ARK ⚜

After the *Haftara* is finished, the reader chants a series of blessings expressing our gratitude for the truth of the Prophets' visions. And then the congregation reads several prayers on behalf of a variety of groups—ranging from fallen martyrs of the past to people who support the operations of synagogues today, from prayers for the political leadership of the United States and Israel to petitions for the safety of the men and women of the American and Israeli militaries. On the Sabbath preceding the beginning of the new lunar month, prayers are also said for a month of "good and blessing." These prayers conclude by our reopening the Ark and returning the Torah scroll to it, while the congregation sings words from the Bible—Psalms, Proverbs, and Lamentations, including these from Numbers:

> *When the Ark came to rest, Moses would say, "Return O Lord, to the myriad thousands of Israel." (10:36)*

So we have both opened and closed the Ark with words that Moses spoke in the desert about the Ark of the Covenant and the tablets in it, on which God had written the Commandments.

The last line sung before the Ark is closed is from Lamentations: "Turn us back, O Lord, to You, and we will return. Renew our days as of old." Rabbi Sacks has a beautiful comment on this sentence: "In Judaism—the world's oldest monotheistic faith—the new is old and the old is new. The symbol of this constant renewal is the Torah, the word of the One who is beyond time."

❧ THE WEEKLY SERMON ❧

In most American congregations, this is the time when the rabbi delivers his weekly sermon. It is certainly an appropriate time since the public reading of the Torah establishes the synagogue as a house of study and the rabbi is traditionally and primarily our teacher. In fact, the word *rabbi* is Hebrew for "my teacher." Moses is called *Moshe Rabeynu*, that is, "Moses our Teacher." The role of the rabbi developed during the Talmudic period of Jewish history when the scholars—

the rabbis—transmitted the Oral Law and answered religious questions about how to apply the Written Torah and Oral Torah to real life situations. In later centuries, great rabbis like Rashi, Maimonides, and Nachmanides wrote commentaries on the Bible and treatises on religious law. They also personally taught their followers how to apply the law to their lives. Much of this teaching occurred on the Sabbath in the synagogue because it was the day when faithful members would not be at work and therefore had more time not just for prayer but for learning. The rabbi was there to do the teaching.

It is only in more recent times, beginning in nineteenth century Germany and spreading throughout the European and American Diaspora, that rabbis emulated their Christian ministerial colleagues and began to deliver sermons from the pulpit at times—such as Sabbath morning—when the greatest number of their congregants was present. There are as many forms and styles of rabbinical sermons as there are rabbis. I have learned much over the years from the sermons of my congregational rabbis, Joseph Ehrenkranz of Agudath Sholom in Stamford, Albert Feldman of the Westville Synagogue in New Haven, Barry Freundel at Kesher Israel in Georgetown, and Daniel Cohen now at Agudath Sholom in Stamford.

Most congregations revere their rabbi, but in some the rabbi's sermons are subjected to what might be called intensive postgame analysis and occasional satire. This has brought forth a whole branch of Jewish humor—rabbi jokes. I will share two with you here, one by a rabbi, the other about a rabbi.

On that Sabbath in 1967, the first after my grandmother died, when I crossed the street to go to Congregation Bikur Cholim in New Haven, the first words I heard the rabbi,

Abraham Hefterman, speak were at the beginning of his sermon after the Torah and *Haftara* had been read:

> Dear congregants, as those of you who have been coming to daily services in the synagogue this week know, and those of you who have not, can now hear, I have a very bad cold and sore throat. It is so bad that I had planned not to give a sermon today, but then I decided that it would not be right for you to derive such pleasure from my misery.

Between Rabbi Hefterman and me, it was love at first joke. The second story is a classic and goes like this:

> The rabbi is about to give his sermon, and the fellow in the front row falls asleep, even before the rabbi starts talking. In fact, he does this every Saturday morning. After weeks of this, the rabbi finally goes over to the man and complains to him: "Why do you fall asleep each week even before I begin my sermon?" The congregant responds, "Because, Rabbi, I have great confidence in you."

When I was fifteen years old, my original rabbi in Stamford, Joe Ehrenkranz, who very positively informed and influenced my religious education and observance, urged me to go to New York to enter a Jewish high school and then from there to enter a seminary and become a rabbi.

As you know, I decided not to, but sometimes I have thought of similarities between the profession I chose and the one I did not. Rabbis, like elected officials, must maintain their credibility with the diverse membership of their congregations, which is their constituency. Public servants, like rabbis, should aspire to be teachers of their constituents and worthy exemplars for them. Both represent and reflect their constituents and also need to lead and uplift them—not simply say what they want to hear. And both clergymen and politicians are ripe targets for humor. On balance, and deservedly, politicians are more often the target of jokes than clergymen. Nevertheless, I still think I made the right career decision for me.

✒ THE *MUSAF* ✒

Our Sabbath morning service now moves to its closing chapter, the *Musaf*, which alludes to the "additional sacrifice." As we have discussed, the *Musaf* service is patterned after the additional communal offering brought on the Sabbath (and other holidays) at the Temple in Jerusalem and has some unique features.

For example, in the *Amidah*, or standing silent prayer, of the Sabbath *Musaf* service, the words from Numbers 28:9–10, which decree the additional Sabbath sacrifices, are recited. With the destruction of the second Temple, prayer has taken the place of sacrifice as the prophet Hosea says so beautifully: "Receive us graciously: so we will offer the words of our lips instead of calves" (14:2).

A second unique feature of the *Musaf Amidah* is that during its holiest part, the *Kedushah*, where we stand tall and strive to emulate the angels bringing Godliness to earth, the *Shema Yisrael* ("Listen, Israel") prayer is added. The rabbis teach that this addition is intended to stress the greater spirituality of the *Musaf*. After echoing the affirmation of faith by the angels— "Holy, holy, holy is the Lord of hosts: the whole world is filled with His glory"—we add our own great human affirmation: "Listen, Israel, the Lord is our God, the Lord is One."

After the *Amidah* is repeated aloud, there is a wonderful tradition that has developed in many synagogues where a group of children come up to lead in the singing of the closing hymns. It is good training for them, and a source of high hope for the future in the rest of us as we conclude the service.

In many synagogues, as the *Musaf* closes, the synagogue president rises to make the "announcements." As with much of Jewish life, the serious and somber can transform unexpectedly into the satirical and humorous. And this is exactly the way some Sabbath morning synagogue experiences have often drawn to a close—with an amateur comedy act, performed by the synagogue president, as he makes announcements.

For years, our president in Georgetown was my college classmate and friend Dr. Michael Gelfand. He was famous— some would say notorious—for drawing out the announcements to as long as fifteen minutes. Mike would mix news of upcoming synagogue services and events, of new members joining the synagogue and of others leaving for the suburbs, with comic patter about it all. He would direct gentle barbs at fellow congregants in the style of a Friars Club roast, and in the same spirit the congregants would call out to him from the pews, humorously complaining about the contents or length of his announcements.

Even some rabbis can't resist closing the Sabbath morning service with humor. One weekend in the 1980s when I was Connecticut's attorney general, Hadassah and I visited the historic Touro Synagogue in Newport, Rhode Island, the oldest surviving synagogue building in America (1763). During the Shabbat morning service, the rabbi called on me, without warning, to chant the *Haftara*. I tried to beg off. You can ask me to give a speech to ten thousand people, and I won't stress out. But ask me to read the *Haftara* before a relatively small congregation on Shabbat without notice and time to prepare, and I'm anxious. But the rabbi insisted and I yielded. Speaking to the *shul* in his own announcements at the end of the service the rabbi said: "I want to thank Attorney General Joe Lieberman for chanting the *Haftara* this morning. For an attorney general, he did a very good *Haftara*."

The synagogue is serious and spiritual, but it is not always a staid place. It's like visiting someone's home where your host wants you to have a good time as well as accomplish the purpose you both share.

With the service concluded, we move now to the totally social, good time of the *Kiddush*—which we have learned to wait for until our morning prayers are done.

❧ SIMPLE BEGINNINGS ❧

❧ Make a regular time for study of the Bible and other works of spiritual inspiration and scriptural interpretation. Start by reading what appeals to you but also consider joining a Bible study group that offers direction. Put yourself on a weekly or daily schedule that takes you through the body of Scripture, or a part of it, in a set period of time.

❧ Be open to the possibility that the passage you study today will have meaning for what is happening in your life that very day.

❧ Make your Bible study a ritualized act. Choose a comfortable or quiet place and try to do your learning there, if possible, each Sabbath.

❧ In studying the Bible, don't just read it as you would the newspaper. Consider the uniqueness of the scriptural text and, of course, its divine origin.

Chapter Seven

THE GIFT OF LEISURE:

HONORING GOD WITH OUR REST

Saturday Afternoon

Very few people know that Joe Lieberman used to be a Baptist," my friend and former Senate colleague Chris Dodd once joked. "But after he was elected and found out how many public events he would have to go to on Friday night and Saturday, he decided to become an Orthodox Jew."

"In fact," Chris added, "I'm thinking of converting to Judaism myself—but only for the weekends."

This was vintage Dodd humor. But in reality the Sabbath is a very communal—if not public—event.

❧ *KIDDUSH* ☙

Now that the morning service has ended, we slowly make our way with our community of friends and fellow congregants to the social hall for *Kiddush*. As at our Friday night dinner, *Kiddush* is the name of the prayer with which we sanctify the wine and the Sabbath. But over the years, it has taken on a broader meaning.

Kiddush is also the name we use for the congregational gatherings after the Saturday morning service, which are the Jewish equivalent of the social hour so many Christians attend after services on Sunday.

My first memories of *Kiddush* as a kid were after Sabbath services in Stamford at the original Agudath Sholom building (now, incidentally, the expanded home of the Faith Tabernacle Baptist Church, where the sanctuary has been kept in beautiful condition and is the same except that the Ark on the altar has been replaced by a baptistery). In the original synagogue, the *Kiddush* was much humbler than it is today in the "new" building up the street. Back then, this prelude to lunch consisted of a few plates of herring, some sweet cakes, and a bottle of blended whiskey. These items and customs were imported from Eastern and Central Europe, the "old country" from which most of the congregants had come. Herring was the "poor man's fish" and the liquor was similarly affordable blended whiskey. My impression was that the shot of whiskey, called "Schnapps" in Yiddish, enjoyed by the "older" men at the Sabbath *Kiddush* was their only encounter with hard liquor each week. For me, growing up in the synagogue, the liquor was off limits and the herring was not yet appealing, so I contented myself with the cake.

Today, the *Kiddush* has become more ample and elegant, in part because of the higher average income of the current congregants and in part because of the cultural and gastronomic influences of the world outside the synagogue in which the congregants have thrived in our magnificently open American society.

So while herring may occasionally still make an appearance on a *Kiddush* table, today you are more likely to find a whole salmon or sablefish, or tuna salad, egg salad, whitefish salad, and/or sushi. Yes, that's right, sushi!

The little "kichel," sugar covered hard crullers, that were featured in my youth may still sometimes appear, but today you are more likely to find layer cakes, brownies, cookies, and in my Stamford synagogue, Ring Dings!

The blended whiskey has been banished, and replaced primarily by a fine array of single malt scotches which, in the past two decades, have become to some as Jewish as bagels and lox. There are still some regional variations in *Kiddush* tastes. For example, our older son, Matt, lives in Atlanta now, and at his synagogue's *Kiddush*, they honor the South and the Sabbath by mostly drinking Bourbon.

Drinking at the Sabbath *Kiddush* is always in moderation, which is certainly what Jewish religious law requires. I have never seen anyone inebriated at a *Kiddush*. But I have found that it surprises a lot of people that there is any drinking at all in a house of worship.

During the winter of 1998, the Senate was going through the impeachment trial of President Clinton. Two of the sessions were scheduled on Saturday, but since the early service at the Georgetown synagogue begins at 7:30 a.m., I was able to pray there, enjoy *Kiddush* briefly, and walk to the Capitol before the trial session began.

When I reached the Senate Chamber on the first of those two Saturdays, my friend Senator Bob Kerrey came over to me and said:

"Joe, this is the Sabbath. Why aren't you in synagogue?"

"Well, Bob," I explained, "my synagogue has an early service. So I stopped on the way to pray with the congregation. I even had enough time to attend the social hour and have a shot of single malt Scotch before walking in."

"Hey Joe," Bob responded, "can I come with you next Saturday? I can't think of a better way to prepare for a president's impeachment trial than a shot of Scotch."

One of the most memorable *Kiddushes* ever for me was held at our house in Washington at the very end of the 2000 national campaign. After the long recount and topsy-turvy court decisions, Al Gore gave an eloquent and patriotic concession speech on a cold Wednesday evening in December. The leaders of our Secret Service detail told me afterward that their customary practice was to stay with the candidate and family they were protecting for just forty-eight hours after the campaign ended and that would mean they would normally leave me on Friday evening. But, they said, they would like to take one more Sabbath morning walk from our house to our synagogue and back, if that was okay with us. Hadassah and I were really touched by this gesture and decided to invite all of the Secret Service agents who had been with us during the campaign to come to our house for a *Kiddush* as soon as they got us home that Sabbath and their professional responsibilities had ended. They were no longer on duty, and we were no longer their protectees.

Through the campaign the men and women of the Service who traveled with our family had become like family to us. So it was wonderful to share a *Kiddush* with them. I said the prayer over the wine and brought out plenty of beer and a bottle of Irish Mist. Toasts were made, and a few tears were shed with a great group of public servants.

My personal experience of the *Kiddush* social today varies depending on whether I'm spending Sabbath in Stamford, in Washington upstairs, or Washington downstairs with the early morning *hashkamah* prayer group. The last of these has a particularly intimate atmosphere. It's just fifty or so members in attendance. The services are held in what is normally a small social hall, so the folding chairs have to be removed and the *Kiddush* table set when the services are over. At this early *Kiddush*, the perhaps surprising focal point is a crock pot of simmering stew, called *cholent*, which is a traditional staple of the Sabbath. Pretty much every Jewish culture around the world has something like *cholent*, because it is one way to deal with the prohibition against cooking on Shabbat. Among Jews from Sephardic (Spanish-Arabic) cultures, it is called *hamin*. The name *cholent* seems to derive from medieval French, meaning *chauldi* (hot) and *lent* (slow). Traditionally, families would prepare their stews on Friday afternoon and leave them in a huge communal oven—often the baker's oven—to cook overnight. That way, a dish of hot food would be ready for lunch on Saturday without anyone having to cook it on the Sabbath.

The most common, traditional recipe for *cholent* includes beef, beans, barley, potatoes, and a kosher sausage, called *kishke*, which is stuffed with goose or chicken fat and flour and not recommended for those concerned about their cholesterol levels. *Cholent* connoisseurs have told me that one test of the quality of *cholent* is if you can clearly distinguish the ingredients from each other—the beef from the potatoes for example or, in vegetarian *cholent*, the carrots from the tomatoes. But after slow cooking for eighteen hours or more, this can be a challenge. One of the sensual delights of the traditional Sabbath is the savory scent of the *cholent* that pervades the home of the *cholent* maker when you wake up on Saturday morning.

For all her Sabbath culinary skills, Hadassah is not a *cholent* aficionado. She finds it to be an excessively heavy dish, one that she boldly claims tends to lower one's energy level and center of gravity.

On the other hand, our sons, Matt and Ethan, have become seasoned *cholent* makers. It is one of the as yet unaccomplished goals of my life to follow in the footsteps of our sons.

During the *Kiddush* at the Georgetown synagogue, after the early prayer group, we are treated to a *cholent* often prepared and always overseen by a leading and learned congregant, Danny Klein. Both he and his *cholent* are treated with considerable respect.

First, the crock pot containing the *cholent,* which has been cooking since before sunset on Friday and is therefore literally steaming, is ceremonially brought from the adjoining kitchen and placed on a piece of white marble that is satirically (and slightly sacrilegiously) referred to as the *mizbayach,* which is the Hebrew word used in the Bible to describe the Temple Altar. Then with the general social buzz of the *Kiddush* as the background chorus, Danny calls people one at a time and in a set order based on his values and determinations alone. Leon Wieseltier, the long-time literary editor of *The New Republic* magazine, is the unordained *"rebbe,"* or rabbi, of this early prayer service. Some even refer to him as its *Kohane Gadol,* or high priest, but this is unofficial and totally sacrilegious. Leon naturally is called by Danny to the *cholent* first and does not demur. When I attend the early morning service, Danny usually calls me up in the "Top Five"—always after a couple of senior and steadfast attendees—and sometimes, I suspect, based on votes I have cast during the previous Senate week. But I am grateful just to be called.

Once I said to Danny, "I appreciate the difficult judgments you so graciously make each week in dispensing the *cholent,* but do you ever take punitive action against anyone through the order of distribution?"

Without hesitation, he responded: "Occasionally, I conclude someone is not behaving as he or she should, and so I don't call them for *cholent* at all in the hope that they won't return."

Stories and jokes about *cholent* have a long and distinguished history. For example in 1850, the great German-Jewish poet Heinrich Heine composed a parody of Schiller's "Hymn to Joy" (famous from the choral part of Beethoven's Ninth Symphony) called "Princess Sabbath." The targets of Heine's satire were German Jews of the nineteenth century who held fast to old customs, like eating *cholent.*

> Cholent, *ray of light immortal!*
> Cholent, *daughter of Elysium!*
> *So had Schiller's song resounded,*
> *Had he ever tasted cholent.*

If I'm in Stamford or attending the later upstairs service at the Georgetown synagogue, the social institution of *Kiddush* looks very different from the early service in Georgetown. For one thing, it's bigger and more crowded. In Washington, the later *Kiddush* can be a madhouse, packed with young people who are working or studying in Washington. The congregation has happily exceeded the capacity of its social hall, and the *Kiddush* sometimes seems like a singles mixer, except of course for us older, long-married members. In fact, our Washington congregation is proud of the large number of matches made at synagogue that have resulted in marriages.

In Stamford, the downstairs minyan holds its *Kiddush* in one of the social halls upstairs, and the atmosphere here is more like a cocktail party for people of all ages. The crowd includes some students who are children of congregants and some retirees, but mostly it is composed of business and professional people who are, broadly speaking, middle aged. There are tables full of all kinds of foods, and adults and children thread their way from the food to their friends and family and back again. The aforementioned Irwin has provided more than one bottle of single malt scotch with the familiar clear plastic thimble-sized shot glasses.

One of the consequences of being a U.S. senator is that you are never fully a private citizen, so at *Kiddush* I am sometimes approached by constituents (in Washington by nonconstituents) with needs that they look to elected officials like me to help satisfy. *Kiddush* is prime time for these kinds of requests. A woman has an immigration problem that perhaps I can assist her with. A man has a son looking for a job in Washington. Can I recommend him? On the Sabbath, I can respond in all truthfulness, "I want to help but I can't write it down now, of course, and I'm worried I will forget, so please call my office on Monday!" I know doctors, too, who are approached at *Kiddush* by people with health concerns. In fact, now that I think of it, Hadassah and I and our kids have often sought medical advice at *Kiddush*.

Being peppered with questions about politics on the Sabbath can feel intrusive (and I'm sure the same is true for medical professionals who are questioned by people like me). That's why it is so helpful that Jewish law actually forbids talking about business on Shabbat. Not that everyone necessarily observes this law, but it is a good guide, and it can be a useful way of diverting a conversation that goes against the spirit of the day. I can smile and say, "But as our tradition teaches, we shouldn't talk about such weekday matters on the Sabbath."

The idea that even our talk should be different on Shabbat than it is on other days goes back to the Hebrew prophets, whose words form an introduction to the text of the *Kiddush* itself that we recite at the beginning of the Sabbath lunch. The prophet Isaiah said:

> If you keep your feet from breaking the Sabbath, and from pursuing your affairs on My holy day, if you call the Sabbath a delight, and the Lord's holy day honorable, and if you honor it by not going your own way or attending to your own affairs, or speaking idle words, then you will find joy in the Lord. (58:13–14)

Avoiding those "idle words"—words about mundane affairs and business concerns of the workweek—enhances the Sabbath experience, making it a true day of peace. Sometimes when Hadassah and I are away from our homes on the Sabbath and go to a synagogue, the rabbi or congregation's president will ask if I would speak about the latest political happenings. I always say, "I wish I could, but as you may know, I don't work on the Sabbath." If they persist and I yield, I repeat my joke about not working, and then speak on a religious—not political—topic.

After the *Kiddush* in Stamford, we either stay for a *shiur* (or Bible class) often taught by my erudite cousin, Harold Bernstein, or we go home. It's too early to have lunch, so we use the time for reading, studying, or talking.

As much as Hadassah and I love entertaining and being entertained at Sabbath meals, the truth is we don't do as much entertaining as we should. This is partly because of my double life, going back and forth from Stamford to Washington, which obliges us to do a lot of traveling on Friday before the Sabbath and makes planning and preparing meals more difficult. But partly, too, it's another consequence of my professional life: being a public servant means being a public person. So Hadassah and I look to *Shabbat* as a sanctuary, offering us the gift of privacy. Remember, I'm the guy with the personal custom of not wearing a watch on Shabbat so I can forget about the pressures of time, normally divided incessantly into fifteen, twenty, and thirty minute blocks that go with my weekday job. The Sabbath is a welcome gift of rest and private time. So Chris Dodd's joke had a lot of truth to it.

❧ SATURDAY LUNCH ❧

The Sabbath meals, as we've already seen, have an order to them. After the *Kiddush* prayer (which we say again before lunch to elevate our meal), we all get up to wash our hands, as we did before dinner on Friday. Once again, this isn't for the sake of hygiene but to spiritualize the act of eating. We aren't merely feeding ourselves as living creatures must do, but preparing for an act of communion with each other and with God. Then we thank God for bringing forth "bread from the earth."

The meal itself follows. Like dinner on Friday, it's a celebratory event, combining plenty of good food with conversation, friendship, laughter, and some talk of the Bible. There is something more intimate about Friday night dinner than Saturday lunch. On Friday night, people are less likely to have guests, more likely to want private time with family. Lunch is different. No one is tired from a day's work and bedtime is still far off, so lunches on the Sabbath give us the freedom of really stretching things out and taking our time, lingering over conversation and courses, dessert, and songs.

Both Friday night dinner and Saturday lunch were wonderful times for Hadassah and me to spend with our children, Matt, Becca, Ethan, and Hani, when they were growing up. Now that they are grown, we also get to spend Shabbat time when they visit, not only with our children but with their spouses, Elizabeth, Jacob, Ariela, and Daniel; and their children, Tennessee, Willie, Abbie, Miriam, Benjamin, Maddy, Camilla, Eden, Yitzhak, Yoav, and Akiva. We have always believed in the importance of making dinnertime a family time, and even at our busiest times, we have tried hard to make sure there were dinners during the week when we were able to sit down together at the table and talk. But no matter how busy we have been, Sabbath dinner and lunch have been guaranteed times when we can catch up with each other and talk and laugh. These are occasions when we parents can try to impart some lessons to our offspring—through word or deed. I cannot adequately express how important Sabbath meals together have been to our family and how much I urge you to put a family meal into your Sabbath if it is not already there. My impression is that the widespread custom of Sunday dinners in Christian families—Protestant and Catholic—has faded. This is a real loss for those families and ultimately for our society.

If you are a member of a community that gathers on the Sabbath, you are fortunate. If you are not, you may want to seek out such a community. Whether it is worship or a hot stew that brings you together, there is something joyful and satisfying about traditions that develop naturally when people get together regularly to do something other than work. The prohibition of driving on the Sabbath ensures that observant Jewish communities develop in close geographic proximity to the synagogue. Since we can't drive, we must walk, and most people don't want to walk long distances. So they tend to live close to one another, which in turn ties the community closer together. There's no reason a church could not adapt and take advantage of this aspect of the Sabbath, encouraging congregants to live close by and even walk to services from time to time.

During the Sabbath lunch, we sing hymns as we did at the Friday night dinner. Well, that's the English word for it, but "hymns" sounds more solemn than they are. The Hebrew word, *zemirot* (singular: *zemer*), means "songs" and calls up in my mind a unique combination of qualities. The tunes are catchy, easy to remember, fast-paced, and lively. So much so that when I'm getting ready for a public appearance or speech, I sometimes catch myself humming a *zemer*. It's not just the words I'm drawing on, but the tune, which uplifts and energizes me.

The poetic words of the *zemirot* are indeed serious, having been composed long ago and far away. Certain *zemirot* are associated with Friday night, others with Saturday, but we sing them pretty much as the mood strikes us, without taking notice of what order we sing them in. For all the seriousness of the lyrics, many Jews (including me) like to have fun with the *zemirot*, substituting the tunes of pop songs for the traditional melodies. One favorite *zemer* of ours is *D'ror Yikra*, whose first line means: "God proclaims freedom to boy and girl, and guards you like the pupil of His eye. . . . Rest and be at ease on the Sabbath day." The song's composer, a tenth-century rabbinic sage, Dunash ben Labrat, also wrote this less peaceful stanza in *D'ror Yikra*: "Crush those who rise against me, zealous God, melting their heart with grief. Then we will open and fill our mouths and tongues with songs of joy to You."

At our family's Sabbath table, these hawkish phrases are often sung—incongruently—to the tune of the 1966 Beach Boys' classic "Sloop John B" ("Drinking all night, Got into a fight, Well I feel so broke up, I wanna go home"). Some Hasidim say that taking a folk melody or pop tune and fitting it into a Sabbath song constitutes an act of spiritual redemption for the melody.

The Sabbath lunch is concluded with the singing of a long grace, preceded by Psalm 126, which, for all its verbal grandeur, I've heard sung to tunes ranging from your favorite college football song to "It's a Small World After all" and Beethoven's Ninth. To me, that seems appropriate because joy and laughter should have an important place in our religious experiences. In fact, Psalm 126 includes the wonderful verse about the joy of the future messianic redemption, "When the Lord brings back the exiles of Zion, we will be like dreamers. Then will our mouths be filled with laughter, and our tongues with songs of joy." As we've discussed, the Sabbath is intended to be a foretaste or preview of that redemption, the experience of the World to Come. Laughter and songs of joy are therefore fitting and proper ingredients of Shabbat!

I would guess that one part of the Sabbath meals may strike our Christian guests as upside down. In Jewish tradition, we thank God for our nourishment not only before but also after the meal. True, we bless God with the *Kiddush* over wine and the prayer over bread, but the formal grace is put off until the meal is completed and we are satisfied by our food. It's natural to be thankful as you sit down to your meal. You're hungry and relieved that the time for satisfying your hunger has come. After we have eaten, we may forget that we have been blessed with plenty; and so our tradition tells us we must take time again to thank God. If your family says grace before meals, you might also want to experiment with this order of doing things and say another prayer of gratitude after. I think you will experience a different level of thankfulness.

🦅 CELEBRATING SABBATH ABROAD 🦅

Given my life as a U.S. senator, Shabbat often turns out a little different from what I've shared here. While the essence of Shabbat and the order of the meals never changes, the setting certainly does. Because the U.S. Constitution tasks the Senate with oversight of foreign relations and national security and because I am a member of the Senate Armed Services Committee, I end up doing a lot of foreign travel. This has created the occasion of some rather exotic backdrops for Sabbath.

When I travel, whether I'm in Madrid or Munich, To-
kyo, New Delhi, Baghdad, or Bogotá, I often ask the local
U.S. Embassy to invite a few Jews from the community to
come visit with me for a Shabbat meal. On these occasions,
I have met some fascinating people. On a Friday night in
New Delhi, for example, I met Lieutenant General J.F.R.
"Jack" Jacob, who is both Indian and Jewish. He is a hero
of modern Indian military history because he led his country's troops into Bangladesh in the victorious 1971 war with
Pakistan. Jacob descends from an old Jewish family that left
Baghdad in the eighteenth century and settled in Calcutta.
As a young man during World War II, horrified by news of
the Nazi Holocaust, he enlisted in the British Army in India
and rose through the ranks. Also present at the meal was another Jewish Indian who could trace his roots in the country
back to the second century when his ancestors were traveling
merchants who came through India and ended up staying for
a very long time.

In Baghdad, I've stayed on the Embassy grounds for Shabbat, hosting my nephew Adam Miller who served three tours
of duty in Iraq with the U.S. Army Military Police Corps.
On one particular Shabbat in Baghdad, we enjoyed great *challahs* from New York thanks to a Jewish Army chaplain and
a wonderful lady from Long Island who sends him a box of
challahs for Jewish soldiers every week. The rabbi conducted
services on Friday night and Saturday morning with more
than forty people from the U.S. Embassy and military in attendance. He highlighted references in the prayer book to the
extraordinary Jewish history in Iraq going back all the way to
the presumed site of the Garden of Eden and the birthplace
of Abraham. Some of the greatest Hebrew prophets are bur-

ied in Iraq at shrines, which incidentally, are honored by the Muslims there.

At lunch that Shabbat, I met with Iraqi Muslim leaders involved with issues of human rights and women's rights. Following lunch, I was honored to receive as my visitor the Iraqi Foreign Affairs Minister, Hoshyar Zebari, a leader of Kurdish Iraqis.

In my travels around the world, particularly on Shabbat, I have been generously and graciously assisted by the worldwide Lubavitch movement, often called by the acronym, CHABAD, which stands for Wisdom, Understanding, and Knowledge. One of the contemporary leaders of this movement, which began in eighteenth century Russia, once said, "Wherever in the world there is Coca-Cola, there should be a Chabad synagogue, school, or center." In recent years, particularly after the passing in 1995 of their charismatic leader, Rabbi Menachem Mendel Schneerson, whose teachings continue to inspire the movement, it appears to me that there are more new Chabad Centers than Coca-Cola franchises opening around the world.

In far-flung places, I have had the honor of attending religious services conducted by Chabad—from Budapest to Beijing, from Taipei to Tashkent, and beyond.

Chabad has also been most generous in providing me and many other travelers with the raw materials of Shabbat—*challahs*, kosher wine, candles, and kosher food.

I will tell you just one of the many stories I could about the resourcefulness of Chabad in carrying out this part of their mission. In February 2004, I was in Munich, Germany, at an international security conference, which John McCain and I attend every year. There were massive anti-Iraq war demonstrations in the city that year to coincide with the conference, which was attended by almost all defense ministers and many foreign ministers of NATO countries. Our American delegation arrived at the hotel where the conference was being held a short time before sunset on Friday. I was greeted by a U.S. military attaché who told me he had had a memorable experience earlier that afternoon:

"As you have seen, Senator, the streets around the hotel are sealed off with riot control vehicles and police cars. A few hours ago, I was called to come out and meet someone. I went out, watched the police vehicles separate, and through them walked a young rabbi with a beard, a black suit, and black hat, carrying a large shopping bag. When we met, he said he had brought the bag for Senator Lieberman for the Sabbath, and here it is."

And there it was, thanks to Rabbi Yisroel Diskin, the Chabad rabbi in Munich—a bag full of all I needed to make and enjoy Shabbat in Munich. How did the rabbi know I was there? My mother, in Stamford, Connecticut, told her Chabad rabbi, Yisroel Deren, that I was going to be in Munich that Shabbat, and Rabbi Deren immediately emailed Rabbi Diskin who took it from there.

❧ A MOST UNUSUAL SABBATH ☙

Occasionally on Shabbat, I have little choice but to be somewhere other than at a Sabbath table. This isn't my preference, of course, but sometimes it's unavoidable. One such occasion occurred at the first inauguration of President George W. Bush, which took place according to the requirements of the

Twentieth Amendment to the Constitution, on January 20, 2001, at noon. For the first time in my memory, Inauguration Day fell on a Saturday. Chief Justice Rehnquist administered the Oath of Office at exactly 12:01. Could I miss this event?

No, I couldn't. I had run for vice president on the ticket that George Bush and Dick Cheney defeated in a bitterly contested election. I knew it was time to come together for the good of the country. Our absence from President Bush's inauguration would be noticed and, not withstanding Shabbat, would be seen by many as divisive and "unsportsmanlike conduct." I knew that Hadassah and I might feel like the ghosts of Christmas past there. Nevertheless, "We gotta go," I told her. Vice President Al Gore was going. We all knew it would have looked like we were ungracious if we did not attend. To make it easier to go to the Capitol for the inauguration, on Friday afternoon we checked into a Capitol Hill hotel, the Phoenix Park. When we got there and saw the Mardi Gras atmosphere among the new president's supporters, we felt very out of place indeed. It was an absolute madhouse. We changed our minds about the hotel. It was not yet sunset, so we hustled home and called our neighbors, Shelly and Mindy Weisel, who welcomed us for Shabbat dinner. We really enjoyed sleeping in the quiet privacy of our own home that night.

The next morning was cold, but we bundled up and made the long journey on foot to the inauguration on Capitol Hill.

As we got close to the Capitol, I heard the roar of thousands of anti-Bush protestors. Were it not for the Sabbath, we would never have found ourselves wading on foot through that crowd. The protesters seemed shocked and thrilled to see us. "Hey, it's Joe Lieberman! Don't give up, Joe," they shouted. There was also, of course, a larger but quieter contingent celebrating the new president's inauguration, who greeted us with respect and good cheer.

Because we had walked and had to wind our way through the crowds, Hadassah and I arrived on the platform after the other senators. One of the first people I saw was Secretary of State Designate Colin Powell, whom I had come to know, like, and respect through my work on the Senate Armed Services Committee.

"So you couldn't get here on time today, Lieberman," Colin said with a big smile.

I knew that Colin Powell had grown up in a Jewish neighborhood in the Bronx and as a result understood and spoke some Yiddish. He and I had previously joked about this little-known biographical fact and particularly about his service as a "Shabbos-goy," a non-Jew who would help his Jewish neighbors by doing something the neighbors were prohibited from doing on the Sabbath, such as turning on a light that had not been turned on before Sabbath or turning up the heat on a colder-than-expected winter day.

So when Colin Powell teased me about being late to the Bush inaugural, I said, "Hey Colin, I thought in your youth you were the best Shabbos goy in the Bronx."

A big smile came across his face, "Oh now I understand your tardiness. Good Shabbos, Senator and Mrs. Lieberman, and thank you for being here on your special day."

After the ceremony was over, Hadassah and I went into the Capitol building and joined some of our Senate colleagues at a reception in the office of the Senate majority leader, Tom Daschle. As we left the reception about fifteen minutes later, we saw Secret Service agents in the hallways, and then the new president of the United States, George W. Bush, who was coming from signing the official document accepting the presidency in the President's Room off the Senate Chamber, a custom that President Reagan began in 1981. President Bush quickly extended a friendly hand to me. It was the first time I had met him.

"Congratulations, Mr. President," I said, shaking his hand.

"Thanks, Senator. And let me congratulate you on the great campaign you ran. I don't think it would have been as close as it was if you had not been on the ticket."

"Thank you, Mr. President," I responded. "Now I look forward to working with you for the good of our country."

"Good," he said, flashing a mischievous smile. "I bet we can find some ways."

At that moment, needless to say, I had no idea how many ways we would find to work together, particularly on the Iraq war, and how much that work would alter the course of my political career. But that is a longer story for another time.

That was, of course, a most unusual Sabbath. Later Hadassah and I had Shabbat lunch in my Senate office, and since it was winter when the sun sets early, we spent the rest of Shabbat on Capitol Hill before getting a ride home when the Sabbath concluded.

❧ PLEASING GOD WITH OUR REST ☙

The Sabbath is not merely about desisting from work, about *not* doing things. In Hebrew, the term for rest, *menucha*, means more than a negation. In the Sabbath liturgy, we pray repeatedly that God will be "pleased with our rest." That means there should be a positive content to our *menucha*, our rest. According to the rabbis, rest was a creation of God. He made it on the first Sabbath. When we work during the week, it should be with a view to creating a space for our *menucha* in emulation of God. We do not use the Sabbath merely as a "breather" to gather strength for our coming labors. We work during the week for the sake of creating our Sabbath rest.

The difference between the work we do the rest of the week and the rest we do on the Sabbath lies in the object toward which each is directed. With our labor during the week, we seek to change and improve the world. With our rest, we seek to change and improve *ourselves* and to renew our relations with God, family, and community and truly feel how much we have to be grateful for.

On a typical Shabbat, the time after lunch is often the best part of the day because it is the most unstructured part of the day. During the summer months when the sun sets later, there are hours to fill with whatever we want—study, reading, conversation, taking a walk, playing catch with our older kids, or taking the younger ones to the neighborhood playground.

And then there is the Shabbat afternoon nap, for which we are also free to choose to use some of our leisure time. A simple nap can be a gift of indulgence. When else do busy people have the time for a nap in the afternoon? It is another way, I believe, in which the Sabbath is a preview of the world to come. And incidentally, it is another opportunity for married couples to enjoy the blessing of being together. For further details I refer you to "Afternoon Delight," a wonderful song from my youth written by Bill Danoff and performed by the Starland Vocal Band.

Shabbat Shalom. I'll see you next at the late afternoon service.

❧ SIMPLE BEGINNINGS ❧

⚜ As the Sabbath nears its halfway point, you may
begin feeling the tug to rejoin the "real" world.
You might feel the seductive call of the shopping
mall, the gym, the office, or the BlackBerry. To
help you resist, make your Sabbath a personal
rule, not an occasional observance. Tell friends
about it rather than letting it be your own private
practice. They might express surprise at first, but
later they may surprise *you* by holding you to your
Sabbath commitment. Disciplines we undertake can
seem difficult at first—they often do—but we get
accustomed to them sooner than we think.

⚜ Try to make your Sabbath conversations different
from that of the weekdays. Elevate your talk. Rather
than gossip, discuss ideas. Seek peace with your
spouse. Avoid talking about business.

⚜ If you had a Sabbath meal at night, try having a
second with your family in the daytime. Most
people want this kind of intimate time together!
Take advantage of the occasion for it that a Sabbath
day offers.

⚜ Do things that require the use of no special
technology and no transportation other than
your own two feet. Take a walk around the
neighborhood or through a nearby park. Visit

neighbors. If you don't know your neighbors, and too many of us do not, get to know them! Make friends of people who live close by to you. You may have to overcome your reluctance to knock on the neighbor's door and introduce yourself, but you—and they—may be grateful that you did.

⌇ At your daytime meal, as at your nighttime one, sing songs!

⌇ For Jews in particular, if you are going to be traveling over the Sabbath and staying in a hotel, you can still enjoy a portable Shabbat just by thinking ahead. It takes planning, but it is very doable. You can arrange for meals ahead of time.

⌇ Consider the *positive* meaning of your rest. It's not just about not working. It is about *filling with meaning* the mental, physical, and spiritual space that is created by your desisting from work.

⌇ Let yourself take an afternoon nap! Enjoy this wonderful, innocent indulgence.

⌇ If you enjoy an occasional beer, wine, or cocktail, then enjoy that on the Sabbath—in moderation, of course. The Sabbath was not given for self-denial, but to enjoy God's world. If you undertake not to drive on the Sabbath, this day may be the ideal time for relaxing with a drink in company with your spouse and/or friends.

Chapter Eight

INTERRUPTING THE SABBATH:

DISCERNING THE GREATER GOOD

<hr>

Now, I am going to interrupt our trip through Shabbat to discuss the times when Shabbat itself can or must be interrupted.

WEIGHING THE CONSEQUENCES

One Sabbath during the spring of 2010, the Southern drawl of Lindsey Graham, my friend and Senate colleague from South Carolina, unexpectedly sounded in my Washington home. The phone had rung and, according to our practice, the answering machine picked it up, allowing me to hear whether the caller was a telemarketer or someone with a more urgent purpose, important enough for me to pick up the phone on the Sabbath.

"Hey, Joe, it's Lindsey. I feel so bad about bothering you on the Sabbath, but I really need to talk with you soon because I am thinking very seriously of pulling off of our energy bill today." Lindsey and John Kerry and I had been working for months to write a bill on energy independence and climate change that would get the sixty votes in the Senate we needed to break the expected filibuster. If Lindsey left, it would make it much harder for us to succeed on this important project. I knew he faced intense pressure from some of his home-state Republicans for "stepping across the aisle" to work with Democrats too often. Lindsey and I had talked about that on Friday, before the Sabbath. He was angry that the Senate Democratic leader, Harry Reid, had just made a surprise announcement that he was going to take up immigration reform soon in the Senate. Lindsey thought that was a political stunt, and told me it would be very hard for him to take on two controversial bipartisan initiatives—energy–climate and immigration reform—at the same time. From his words on my answering machine that Saturday, I knew that our energy–climate proposal faced an imminent and perhaps fatal crisis. So, I picked up the phone to try to dissuade Lindsey from withdrawing, thereby violating the Sabbath.

I needed to make a quick decision, and I did—based on my judgment of how much I believed was at stake if our energy–climate bill didn't pass. I also based my decision on years of reading and discussing with rabbis and others the occasions when Sabbath-observant Jews have been permitted or required to ignore the normal prohibitions of the Sabbath because a greater good, such as preserving or protecting life and health or supporting the well-being of the community, was on the line.

As long ago as the Talmudic period, the rabbis recognized that there were some actions that were greater than even Sabbath observance because they upheld fundamental values that the Sabbath itself was meant to honor.

The first of these is *pikuach nefesh*, which means "saving a life." The Talmud teaches, "We tend to matters involving [danger to] life on the Sabbath [even when doing so makes it necessary to desecrate the Sabbath]. One who is quick [to desecrate the Sabbath in order to save a life] is praiseworthy, and he does not need to obtain authorization from the [rabbinic] court" (*Yoma* 84b).

In support of this principle, a sage of the Talmud, Rabbi Shimon ben Menasya, quotes the verse, "The children of Israel shall keep the Sabbath, to observe the Sabbath throughout their generations" (Exodus 31:16). The rabbi then explains: "The Torah said: 'Violate one Sabbath on his account [by saving his life] so that he may [live to] observe many Sabbaths'" (*Yoma* 85b).

Still another rabbi, Rav Yehuda, derives support for this idea from Leviticus: "You shall therefore keep My statutes, and My judgements: which if a man do, he shall live in them: I am the Lord" (18:5). We learn from this that we should expect to "live in them," God's laws, not die by them. Therefore we violate the Sabbath to save a life. Religion is all about how we live and make life better."

The Sabbath can also be broken to protect life from attack. Josephus, the Jewish historian of the period, writes that in first century Babylonia a pair of Jewish brothers, Anilaeus and Asinaeus, led an army of Jewish supporters in a revolt against the ruling Parthian Empire, based in what is today Iran. The empire's forces attacked the Jewish rebels on the Sabbath, assuming they would not take up arms to fight back and defend themselves on their holy day. They were wrong. When attacked on Shabbat, the brothers and their backers fought and won important victories. And that response would be approved by rabbinic tradition. Under such circumstances, breaking the Sabbath isn't merely an option but a commandment, in order to protect life.

There are other examples of Talmudic exceptions to Sabbath requirements because they protect the well-being of the community, not just to save human life.

For example, in the time of the Roman Empire, the rabbis warned Jews not to frequent the amphitheaters and circuses because these were often places of idol worship and public immorality. On the Sabbath, indulging in such entertainment would clearly be unacceptable. But the rabbis of the time also held that if there were matters of community concern that needed to be discussed with the wider community of Romans and their leaders, and those discussions were most likely to occur in the amphitheaters or circuses, then Jews could go to such civic assemblies, even on the Sabbath.

There are similar ancient rabbinic rulings that gave flexibility in some religious observances to individuals who were, in the Talmud's words, "close to the government." The Talmud describes the case of a Jewish man, Avtolos, son of Reuben, whom the rabbis permitted to cut his hair in the manner of the Romans—although that was generally prohibited among the Jews of that time—because Avtolos was "close to the government." If cutting his hair enabled him to mingle more freely with influential leaders, even though they were pagans, he might be able to save lives or better protect the welfare of his community.

These Talmudic examples come from periods of history when Jews lived insecure lives under dictatorial governments. Today, for us as free people in great democracies like the United States and Israel, the circumstances are very different. Of course there are new challenges that go along with new freedoms and new power. The modern State of Israel, immediately upon being founded, faced questions about how to defend the lives of its citizens while respecting the Sabbath. I recently wrote to Israel's Chief Rabbi, Yona Metzger, who is responsible for the country's Ashkenazic (or European Jewish) community, to ask how this balance has been struck. Rabbi Metzger kindly wrote back, citing a variety of authoritative rabbinic sources from ancient and recent times that are consistent with the ones I cited above. Of particular interest to me were his comments on how army rabbis, from himself on down, give counsel to the Israel Defense Forces regarding the standards they should apply to their decisions about how to defend the country on the Sabbath. Even small divisions of soldiers and elite groups may seek the advice of an army rabbi in this role. "On a practical level," writes Rabbi Metzger, "the laws of the army prohibit the desecration of Shabbat that is not for the sake of saving lives or for current security needs."

As for government functions, Rabbi Metzger points out that from the state's founding, Israel's parliament, the Knesset, has been closed on Shabbat. Individual members of the Knesset and cabinet ministers may sometimes need to travel or use phones on Shabbat in order to discuss important security matters, and they do so with the advice of their own local rabbis as the need arises.

For myself and many others today, the Talmudic precedents provide the basis for making exceptions to normal Sabbath observance when an opportunity arises to do something that may not directly save a life but is related to its protection, preservation, and enhancement. Today there is fortunately no need to go to the "amphitheaters or circuses," only to fulfill our official responsibilities in free countries.

So that's why I picked up the phone when I heard Lindsey Graham's voice that Sabbath afternoon. In an instant, I weighed the violation of Sabbath I would commit by using the phone against the greater protection of our security and environment if the caller on the phone helped us pass energy independence–climate legislation. For me, the choice was clear. I had to minimize the risks.

Later that afternoon, John Kerry flew back to Washington and, after checking with my staff, came right to my house from the airport. "Shabbat Shalom," John said when I opened the door. "I am really sorry to bother you on the Sabbath." I reassured him that it was no bother and that he had done exactly the right thing in coming over to my house. We both knew that the withdrawal of our leading (and still lone) Republican co-sponsor could be fatal to our bill. Kerry and I have known each other since we were at Yale together in the 1960s. In 1987, he was chairman of the Democratic Senate Campaign Committee and was one of the people who convinced me to run for the Senate. Since then we had disagreed on some big foreign policy issues— like the Iraq war—and I was one of the several candidates for the Democratic nomination for president whom John Kerry defeated in 2004, but this energy-climate legislation had given us an opportunity to work together for something big and also rekindled our personal friendship. On that Shabbat afternoon, we sat together in my living room over coffee and soda and talked about what we could do to keep Lindsey on our bill and, if we failed to do that, how we could still pass the bill.

As it turned out, Senator Graham announced later that day that he would suspend his work with John Kerry and me. For that reason and others, although Kerry and I tried hard and had a lot of help, our legislation never got enough votes to pass. Notwithstanding the result, I have no regrets about taking Lindsey's phone call on the Sabbath because I knew how important his involvement was to our energy independence–climate legislation and how important our legislation was to our country, and therefore, I knew I had to try to keep Lindsey involved.

❧ CHOOSING BETWEEN LIFE AND LAW ❧

By honoring the Sabbath, we celebrate God's creation. It would make no sense if honoring the Sabbath stopped us from taking action to protect God's creation. In the choice between life and religious law, God-given life must triumph because its sanctification is the overriding purpose of the religious laws. Very often when I have to make a decision about whether to act on the Sabbath, I don't know to what extent life, security, or community well-being are on the line. So I have to make a judgment call that minimizes the risk. That is what Jewish tradition teaches me. When a Sabbath-observant doctor gets in his car on the Sabbath to drive to the hospital to help a patient, he doesn't know whether he will be successful in saving the patient's life. He knows that he must go and try, and that effort—even more than his Sabbath observance—honors God and His creation.

You can imagine many obvious scenarios where people who are not doctors would not hesitate to break Shabbat. I know plenty of Sabbath-observant people who, when faced with a medical emergency, have jumped into the car or an ambulance to rush a sick child or a mother in labor to the hospital. Situations like these require no special discernment to make that judgment call. Some may not be so clear but are still compelling.

I remember, a few years ago in Washington, a bitterly cold Saturday in February after a big snow storm had left a lot of ice on the ground. Afternoon votes were scheduled in the Senate that Shabbat, so Hadassah and I went to synagogue early together and I was going to walk in to the Capitol from there while she walked home with neighbors. After services, Hadassah decided she didn't want me to walk with only my Capitol police escort for company. So we began our stroll along M Street with the two officers following. Hadassah stepped on a patch of ice, slipped, and fell down hard. Landing on her wrist, she cried out in pain. Her hand seemed limp.

My heart and head moved me reflexively and quickly to call over the Capitol police car and get right in to take Hadassah to the hospital. I knew a fall and injured wrist were not likely to be life threatening, and I suppose we could have walked to the hospital. But my wife was clearly in real pain and needed to be seen by a doctor as soon as possible. How could I have decided that my Sabbath religious observance prohibited me from staying with my injured wife and facilitating her treatment? I knew I couldn't.

We went by car to the George Washington Hospital where

the doctors found that Hadassah had broken her wrist and they put it in a cast. A few days later, they decided the cast wasn't doing the job, so they operated and reset her wrist.

Not every observant Jew would have made the decision I did. I understand and respect that difference. But I have had no second thoughts about the decision I made.

❧ IMPORTANT DISTINCTIONS ❧

Deciding whether to accompany Hadassah to the hospital was a private decision. In my public life, some of the decisions I have made about whether to do something I normally wouldn't do on the Sabbath have been easy, and some have been more difficult.

When I began my political career as a state senator in the early 1970s, I developed broad personal guidelines for the Sabbath based on my understanding of religious law. I would not do "politics," but I would carry out time-sensitive government responsibilities that no one else could do. In other words, I distinguished between politics and government. A lot of political events occur on Friday night and Saturday, particularly when you are campaigning in an election year. But, even when you're not, there are always testimonial dinners, community meetings, and social events on the Sabbath that I would normally attend if held during the week. At first, some people were puzzled and some were even angry when I didn't show up at their events. But when they realized I was not attending for religious reasons and that I was following this practice consistently on Friday evenings and Saturdays, they accepted, respected, and often said they admired my Sabbath observance. I hope that sends a message of encouragement to young, religiously observant people of any faith that their observance will not be a problem in American politics. It also says much to all of us about the values of the American people.

Sometimes, I even think my Sabbath observance may actually have helped my political career, although of course, I did not become Sabbath observant because of a focus group or public opinion poll. For that, I must "blame" my parents and rabbis.

Here's a story that illustrates my point. In the state senate, I had a Democratic colleague and friend named Con O'Leary, who later became the Senate majority leader. One day in 1988, during my first run for the U.S. Senate, against the incumbent Republican senator Lowell Weicker, Con called and said to me, "Joe, I think you're going to win this election."

"That's great, Con," I said, knowing most people felt otherwise. "Why?"

"I went to visit my mother yesterday," he explained, "and three of her lady friends were with her having afternoon tea. So you had four silver-haired Catholic ladies there. I asked them who they planned to vote for in the presidential race. They said they were going to vote Republican—for Bush, not Dukakis. I argued with them, but I finally gave up and said, 'What about the Senate—Weicker or Lieberman?' And my mother said, 'That's easy, I'm voting for Lieberman.' All the other women said, 'Yes, we're voting for Lieberman.'"

"Why is that such an easy choice?" O'Leary asked his mother.

And Mrs. O'Leary said, "I like the fact that Joe Lieberman is a religious man and keeps his Sabbath."

"And," Con concluded, "the three other silver haired heads nodded."

Thank you Mrs. O'Leary.

Practical problems of Sabbath observance were few during my state senate and attorney general service, though when they did come up there was usually no need to resort to Sabbath breaking. In my very first session in the state senate in 1971, when I was only twenty-seven years old, the senate was divided closely between Democrats and Republicans, nineteen to seventeen, so literally every vote counted. There was a Republican governor and a Republican lieutenant governor, so in a tie vote, the lieutenant governor would break the tie. We generally had long debates about the budget, and that year, it was a particularly tough situation. Finally, there was an agreement on the budget late on Friday night—and I had already gone home for Shabbat. The majority leader, Ed Caldwell, understood that I couldn't come back until after sundown—so they sent someone down to the house in New Haven to tell me what happened and that I should be ready to come back after sundown on Saturday. I did and the budget passed. *The Bridgeport Post* told the story with the brilliant headline: "Butch Caldwell and the Sundown Kid."

When I served as state attorney general, my deputies were under instructions to contact me in the event of an emergency on the Sabbath. But they and I can't remember a time they had to. One Saturday, an occasion arose involving the state police. My staff consulted with each other by phone and decided they could handle it without involving me. Because we had discussed similar situations, they knew what I would do and did it. At responsible levels of government, decisions like these can be handled through prior planning. Perhaps one part of God's purpose in giving us the Sabbath was to cultivate precisely these qualities of forethought in us.

The most public time my Shabbat observance was a factor in my Connecticut political life was in 1988 when I was running for the U.S. Senate. Going into the convention, I knew I had enough votes to win the Democratic nomination, but I couldn't go to the convention because it was—as had always been the case—on a Saturday. So I pretaped my acceptance speech. On the day after, the front page of many of the state's newspapers showed me on the big screen at the convention in a photograph of the video we had taped. The headline noted that I had accepted the nomination by a prerecorded speech because I was observing the Sabbath.

The move from state to national level politics came with new challenges. In the state senate, votes on Friday night or Saturday were rare. In the U.S. Senate, they are more common. When a U.S. senator votes, it may literally mean life or death to other people. The most obvious example of this is a Senate resolution to go to war, but there are many other votes that affect public health and safety, and the "general welfare" of the community.

So I have never hesitated to engage in meetings, debates, or votes or to take calls regarding national or homeland security on the Sabbath. That happened first during the debate and vote in 1991 about whether to authorize President George H. W. Bush to go to war to push Saddam Hussein's Iraqi forces out of occupied Kuwait. The debate and vote concluded on a Saturday afternoon. I walked into the Senate and fully participated in the debate and vote. Because most of the Senate Democrats were opposed to or ambivalent about going to war against Saddam Hussein and I was strongly and publicly supportive, the Bush Administration had asked me to be the lead Democratic cosponsor of the authorizing resolution with my Republican colleague and friend, Senator John Warner of Virginia. It was a good and heated debate. In the end, the resolution passed, but only by five votes, fifty-two to forty-seven. Three senators voting differently would have altered history—in my opinion greatly for the worse. I believed deeply that our national and economic security were on the line in that debate and vote, and I therefore believed my professional and moral responsibility to participate overrode traditional Sabbath restrictions.

I had a more difficult Sabbath decision to make a little later that same Sabbath day. An aide to Senate Majority Leader Bob Dole came over to me on the Senate floor shortly after the vote on the resolution and said, "The Leader wants you to come to his office right now." I said, "No problem," and walked quickly with him to Dole's grand office about fifty feet from the Senate Chamber. Bob had a phone in his hand and said, "I am calling President Bush to notify him of the vote, and I wanted you to be here." I thanked him for his courtesy and told him I was grateful to be there. It was, after all, an historic moment.

When President Bush came on, Senator Dole reported the vote to the commander in chief, said it was close, but the president now had clear and strong authority to take military action against Saddam Hussein, and he was confident that most of the Congress and the country would unite behind him and behind our military. Then Bob Dole said, "Mr. President, I have Senator Lieberman here with me. I wanted him here because we could not have passed this resolution without his support." Pause. "Of course, Mr. President,"

Dole said and handed me the phone. Now I know I could have said, "Sorry, Bob, I don't use the phone on Saturday except in an emergency." But I had already left the normal Sabbath path for the debate and vote, and I knew there were many rabbinical rulings over the centuries urging respect for a head of state, particularly in time of national crisis. I took the phone and said, "Good afternoon, Mr. President." The president graciously thanked me for my support and work on the resolution. He said he knew that most Democrats had voted "no," but he also knew the resolution would not have passed without the support of the ten Democrats who had voted "aye" and that he especially appreciated all I had done to make it bipartisan.

I thanked him and added that I knew the authority given to him by the resolution was great, and I supposed—notwithstanding how important I believed it was that Iraq's invasion of Kuwait be turned back—there were some presidents I would hesitate to give such broad authority. But in this case, I had every confidence that he would use this authority wisely and well. I gave the phone back to Bob Dole, who said goodbye. I thanked Bob and walked back to my Senate office where I said the Sabbath afternoon and evening prayers and waited until I could be driven home.

Budgetary decisions on matters such as health care for seniors and children can also have serious implications for people's lives and health. Arguably, a senator's responsibility to vote on the Medicare budget on the Sabbath is like a doctor's responsibility to treat a patient covered by Medicare on the Sabbath. In Sabbath law, doctors are not just permitted, but required, to break Shabbat for their patients. I have not asked a rabbi for an opinion on whether a senator voting on Medicare is also mandated to break the normal Sabbath restrictions, but I have discussed it enough with rabbis and thought about it enough to know that I would. In fact, I have.

❧ PERSONAL CONVICTIONS ❧

When I arrived in Washington in 1989, Hadassah and I joined the Georgetown synagogue, whose rabbi, Barry Freundel, had also just recently arrived.

I met with Rabbi Freundel to discuss the intersection of my senatorial duties with my Sabbath observance. We agreed at the outset that I was not asking him to issue a rabbinical opinion for me on any particular Sabbath-related scenario. I was only seeking his general guidance, and that was what he himself wished to give. I wanted his knowledge of Jewish law, values, and history to inform the decisions I knew I would have to make myself. And they have.

In the end, we each have to interpret the Torah for ourselves, doing what seems right. In deciding what is right, I have, however, depended on the decisions of those who went before me and sought the counsel of those more learned than I. In the end, I have always believed that God wants us to be personally responsible, not to hand our moral responsibility for making decisions over to someone else.

So Rabbi Freundel discussed with me the considerations I should take into account when faced with a decision. For instance, he gave me some guidelines for deciding how to get to the Capitol on the Sabbath or a festival. If I decide I must attend to my government responsibilities on the Sabbath, he suggested a hierarchy of ways to do so, based on the urgency and consequences of my participation. First, if possible, I should walk to the Capitol, which would not violate Shabbat at all. Second, I could use a pre-purchased ticket for the Washington Metro and take the train, since it was going anyway. Third, I could ask a non-Jewish staff member to drive me. Fourth, I might decide to drive myself if there was no alternative and the consequences of not going to the Capitol would greatly affect human life or national security.

As it turned out, only twice in my senatorial career, thus far, have I felt I had to get into a car on Shabbat to go to the Capitol. On all other occasions, I foresaw the problem and walked or stayed overnight at the Capitol. During one of the big budget debates and gridlocks of the Clinton Administration, I had worked with a bipartisan group of senators to put together and propose a budget that would bring the federal books back in balance. On Shabbat, no votes were expected, so I was home; but the senators were in town awaiting results of negotiations on the budget. One of my staff members came to the house and told me that Senator John Chafee of Rhode Island had called and said there was to be an important and urgent last-minute meeting between some of the leaders of our bipartisan balanced-budget group and representatives of the Administration. Chafee thought it was important that I be there. I got in the car, and a staff member who was not Jewish drove me in. With so much on the line for our country, I felt I had a responsibility to go. It was a constructive, though not determinative, meeting—one of many that eventually led to the enactment of the Balanced Budget Act of 1997.

The other occasion was a crucial moment in negotiations in 2004 when my colleague Senator Susan Collins of Maine sent a staff member to my house on a Saturday to tell me there was an unexpected crisis in the work we had been doing to adopt the legislative recommendations of the 9/11 Commission. I was driven to the Capitol and participated in meetings that were determinative and that led to the biggest reorganization of America's national security agencies since the aftermath of World War II.

On several occasions I have taken phone calls on the Sabbath. My general rule is that if any official in the federal government—particularly one involved in security—feels he or she needs to talk with me on Shabbat about a matter that he or she deems to be time sensitive and requires my response, I will take the call. If the person calls my office or staff about reaching me, my staff will tell the caller's staff that I will take the call on the Sabbath if it requires my personal attention and is time sensitive. If not, I would prefer to wait. If they have any doubt, I will take the call. On a few occasions, my staff has told the caller's staff that if the matter is not urgent but the caller doesn't want to wait and can come over to my house, I would be glad to talk in person, as I did with John Kerry that Saturday afternoon.

One Friday night in December 2004, during the administration of President George W. Bush, I took a call from his chief of staff Andy Card. When I heard Andy's name on the answering machine, I picked it up. It turned out to be a time-sensitive matter concerning homeland security, which required a reaction from me personally, so I was glad I took it. President Bush had nominated former New York City police commissioner Bernie Kerik to serve as secretary of homeland security. But now, a week later, Kerik was withdrawing under a legal and ethical cloud. The president urgently wanted to know if I would consider being nominated as a replacement for Kerik. Andy and I talked about it. In the end I asked him to thank President Bush for considering me, but I was not ready to leave the Senate.

I've served since 2007 as chairman of the Senate Committee on Homeland Security and Government Affairs and in that capacity sensitive matters requiring my personal attention often come up. President Obama's first national security adviser, General Jim Jones, called me one Saturday about a national security question but waited until it was after dark when Shabbat was over. When he told me that he had not wanted to interrupt my Sabbath, I thanked Jim for his respect but asked him never to hesitate on such a matter again if he felt it was important that he talk to me during the Sabbath.

Sometimes my system of listening to the answering machine on the Sabbath works imperfectly. In the perfect system, I would ask what the person is calling *about*, but of course, I can't. On a Friday night in 1989, Hadassah and I were home in Washington having Shabbat dinner. The phone rang and the voice on the answering machine announced it was Vice President Dan Quayle calling. I decided quickly that, although I didn't know what he was calling about, if the vice president of the United States wanted to talk with me, I could assume it was important, so I picked up. It turned out that VP Quayle was just calling to thank me for a speech I had given. Well, better that I erred on the side of caution than ignore a possible unknown emergency situation.

When I ran for vice president in 2000, and for president in 2004, I followed my personal rule of no politics on the Sabbath, but during 2000, there were a lot of questions about what I could and could not do on Saturday if I ended up as vice president of the United States. Being a senator is one thing. Being a heartbeat away from the Oval Office is quite another. I've noted already in an earlier chapter that the Sabbath is intertwined with the history of the presidency. Many American presidents have observed the Sabbath in their way, but that was before modern weaponry, terrorism, and global economic realities made the decisions of the chief executive incomparably more time sensitive, potentially down to the split second.

When Al Gore selected me as his running mate, some questioned my ability to fulfill the responsibilities of the vice-presidency on the Sabbath. President Bill Clinton told me at the beginning of that campaign to ignore anyone who doubted my capacity to help the campaign six days a week and, if elected, be on the job every day. I laughed out loud when Clinton said, "Just tell them to go straight to Hell!"

The issue of my observing the Sabbath if we won was understandable and got serious attention. Before I was even nominated, Matthew Rees in the *Weekly Standard* observed that the Sabbath laws "would provoke questions about [Lieberman's] ability to govern in the event he became president." In *Slate* magazine, Judith Shulevitz explained the exemptions granted for protecting human life and attending to the needs of the community, and she concluded that, if elected, I would have no problem carrying out the duties of the vice president on the Sabbath.

The lesson I hope you will take away from this discussion is the priority Jewish law and tradition gives the sacred mission of saving, protecting, and preserving life, even where the threat is not immediate or yet definitive. One is obligated to act even when the cost is temporarily overriding God's holy Sabbath.

Rabbi Chaim Soloveitchik (1853–1918), a revered Lithuanian rabbi and grandfather of Rabbi Joseph Soloveitchik, was known for his leniency in permitting Jews who were feeling ill to eat on the solemn holiday of Yom Kippur. Normally the Day of Atonement is marked by fasting all day long, abstaining from all food and water. In theory, only a threat to life permits one to eat. Rabbi Soloveitchik was similarly lenient about giving permission to sick people to break Shabbat rules. Someone asked him once why he did not treat Yom Kippur and Shabbat more strictly, and Rabbi Soloveitchik responded, "I am not lenient in regard to Yom Kippur or the Sabbath. I am stringent in the *mitzvah* [commandment] of guarding life."

That is the standard I try to follow whenever my public responsibilities conflict with my Sabbath observance. To do otherwise, it seems to me, would be to put form over substance, to elevate the law above the values on which the law is based, and to forget that the Sabbath is primarily a day to affirm and uphold the life that God has given us.

Now we can and will return to our regular Shabbat schedule.

❧ SIMPLE BEGINNINGS ❧

❧ Remember that God gave the Sabbath to enhance our lives, not to endanger our welfare. Therefore when you decide you must interrupt the Sabbath for a higher purpose, don't see this as a desecration of the holy day but rather as another *commanded* feature of it. God commands us to observe the Sabbath, but when circumstances demand, He wants us to stop our rest and do what needs to be done, such as protecting life and health, defending our security, and helping others with urgent needs.

❧ The primary circumstance that calls for interrupting the Sabbath is protection of life, even where the danger is only hypothetical and not certain. About the protection of life we must be hypervigilant.

❧ The Sabbath is an excellent time to meditate on the sanctity of life.

❧ If you incorporate Sabbath observance as a regular feature of your week, take some time to think over the unique circumstances under which you would break the Sabbath. You might even write down on a piece of paper what you come up with. It's very uncomfortable to be taken by surprise and have to make an on-the-spot decision without a predetermined, clear set of standards and priorities for setting aside the Sabbath. Decide

this for yourself, and consult a spiritual mentor if
appropriate—it's well worth the investment of time
and thought.

In coming up with your guidelines for breaking
the Sabbath, think in terms of contingencies and
preferences. Some acts of Sabbath breaking intrude
less on the holiness of the day than others. If
possible, those should be preferred over acts that
more broadly undermine the spirit of rest.

Chapter Nine

LEAVING THE SABBATH:

MAKING WISE DISTINCTIONS

Saturday Evening

Have you ever attended a reunion—a class reunion, or maybe a family reunion? If so, you know that what begins with pleasurable anticipation and leads to real enjoyment often ends on a melancholy note, as everyone realizes that it's going to be some time before they see each other again. The same is true of joyous family affairs like weddings. People often stick around for a while after the formal activities have concluded. They don't want to leave. In fact, when Hadassah and I got married—each for the second time—we anticipated that feeling, and instead of rushing right off after the reception, we invited about fifty family members and friends back to my parents' house for a couple of hours to share wedding stories and open presents.

The weekly meeting of our "Shabbatland" community is a reunion of sorts that we know will not come around again for another week. That's not a long time, yet as Shabbat draws to a close, we experience a certain apprehension mixed with the desire to make the most of these last couple of hours of Sabbath rest. This sadness upon leaving is a tribute to the special sweetness of Shabbat.

The concluding hours of the Sabbath are only in part melancholy. They are mostly spiritual and profoundly hopeful. We believe that on the Sabbath we are closer to God; in fact, we believe we are visited by God. So as the Sabbath ends, we have our last special opportunity to connect with Him before the tranquility of the day of rest gives way to the hubbub of daily life. In the afternoon service, called *Mincha*, we begin with prayers, then we have a ritual third meal called *Seudah Shlishit*, and finally we share in the regular evening prayers and the candlelit departure ceremony, *Havdalah*, in which we bid farewell to the Sabbath.

As the sun begins to set on a typical Saturday afternoon, when I'm in Stamford, I head back to synagogue. In Washington, where the walk to synagogue for the second time in one day can feel discouragingly long, I typically stay home. I miss the *shul* community, but I love spending the extra time with Hadassah and whichever of our children and grandchildren are with us.

"Shabbat Shalom" along with the Yiddish *"Gut Shabbos!"* ("Good Sabbath!") are the standard Sabbath greetings from just before the day of rest arrives on Friday afternoon until its departure on Saturday evening. Literally, *Shabbat Shalom* should be translated as "Sabbath of Peace" or "Peaceful Sabbath." But *shalom* means more than the absence of war or other communal or personal conflicts. It means more than just a feeling of restfulness. In Hebrew, it connotes wholeness, completeness. It is hard to feel at peace if you don't feel whole.

When we sense we are missing something in our lives, we are uneasy, restless, anxious—the opposite of *shalom*, the opposite of Shabbat.

As we discussed earlier, through the Sabbath's three major services—Friday night, Saturday morning, and Saturday afternoon—we experience a retelling and a foretelling of sacred history. Our Friday prayers affirm our faith in God as Creator. On Saturday morning, the focus switches to revelation—the giving of the Torah and the Ten Commandments to Moses at Mt. Sinai, and with it man's purpose and destiny. Now on Saturday afternoon, we look to the future redemption, the result of all our efforts to partner with God in "fixing" the world, to make it and ourselves whole.

❧ THE PROMISED REDEMPTION ❧

Jews and Christians alike recognize the world's brokenness and the ultimate remedy of that condition in the coming of Messiah. For Jews it will be the first time, for Christians it will be the second, but I believe we are all praying for and working together with God toward the same goal and for the same reasons. When God created the world, He recognized it as "good." Only on the sixth day of creation, when all was complete, did He call the world "very good." By eating from the Tree of Knowledge, Adam and Eve sinned and created a breach in this primordial wholeness. The world was no longer "very good," it was merely "good," as sin and evil competed with and confused themselves with virtue and good. Redemption is the moment when God restores creation to its earlier moral height, assuring us that all the travails and sufferings of human experience were not, after all, meaningless. We all know that good people often suffer while evil goes unpunished. In the future, all will be put right. We'll see that everything that went before was building to a conclusion that will enable us to understand the tragedies and enigmas of old. This promised redemption is our guarantee of a future wholeness, and assures us that our lives, even now, are meaningful and "whole" from God's perspective. On the Sabbath, we have the time—and the open mind and spirit that comes with time—to contemplate this larger vision of human history and destiny with its promise of ultimate meaning. And on the Sabbath, we have the time and openness to experience a taste of this future redemption, a preview of what is to come.

Redemption is a central theme of the Sabbath afternoon, and the liturgy prompts us to meditate on it. We read from Isaiah about how "a redeemer will come to Zion, to those of Jacob who repent of their sins" (59:20). In the *Alenu* prayer, we embrace Zechariah's prophecy: "The Lord shall be King over all the earth; on that day the Lord shall be One and His name One" (14:9).

Mystical tradition tells us that the Sabbath afternoon service is particularly favored by God, who listens to prayers as the day ends with a special openness and receptivity because He too will miss the closeness Sabbath gives Him to His creations. King David must have had this time of day on the Sabbath in mind when he wrote in the Psalms, "As for me, may my prayer come to You, Lord, at a time of favor. O God, in Your great love, answer me with Your faithful salvation" (69:14). That verse from Psalm 69 is also read at the Saturday afternoon *Mincha* service.

❧ SANCTIFYING GOD'S NAME ❧

In the afternoon *Amidah*—the silent, standing prayer—we ask God, "May Your children recognize and know that from You comes their rest, and through their rest, they will sanctify Your name." That sentence moves me every Shabbat afternoon because it envisions our Sabbath rest not just as the fulfillment of a command but as the sanctification of God's name, the ultimate in service to God. I understand the sentence to mean that by observing the Sabbath we are declaring our faith in God as our Creator and eternal Sustainer, and we are making that declaration—sanctifying God's name—to and for the entire world.

The other thought this prayer evokes in me is how good God is that He calls us to sanctify His name by resting. By accepting His gift of rest, we sanctify His name. That is a very good exchange!

❧ SWEET FELLOWSHIP ❧

In Stamford, when we finish the afternoon prayers, we proceed to the social hall for the third Sabbath meal. In Washington, we go to our kitchen table at home. At both, we say again the prayer over the *challah* bread. This time, however, they are usually smaller *challah* rolls, and the meal consists of light salads. In Stamford, one of the rabbis or a visiting scholar or a congregational member will lead a discussion of a biblical or Talmudic text.

At our home table, Hadassah and I and our family will either discuss some ideas we took away from the morning's Torah reading or together read and discuss a very special book in the Mishnah called *Pirkei Avot*, "Ethics of the Fathers," which incorporates wise statements from over two hundred rabbis who lived and taught in Talmudic times. In the synagogue or in our home at the Saturday afternoon meal, we always sing the twenty-third psalm to a haunting, hopeful melody that captures the feeling of that moment of the Sabbath. The words are familiar to almost everyone and seem to fill the gaps in our personal "wholeness" with words of divine support.

Before Hadassah and I moved back to Stamford in 2007, we lived for almost twenty-five years in the Westville neighborhood of New Haven, where a lot of other observant Jewish families lived. Years before we moved there, the neighbors formed a "Shabbat group" that met in the house of a different member each Saturday afternoon to study, pray, and socialize. Attendance ranged from ten to forty, depending on who was in town that weekend. Over the years, Hadassah and I and our children had some of our most substantive, spiritual, and enjoyable Shabbat experiences with this group of New Haven neighbors and friends. The fact that all this happened in someone's home reminds us that a strong Sabbath community can sometimes be formed and found outside a formal house of worship.

The New Haven Shabbat group was a mix of doctors, lawyers, Yale professors, visiting Israeli academics, business people, spouses, and children. The kids would play, and the parents would study and pray together. I can still feel that mellow twilight atmosphere as we gathered around a table in someone's dining room or living room. Each Saturday, a different member would lead a discussion of the week's Torah reading, which led, as *divrei Torah* ("words of Torah") often do, to wider discussions of values, history, and life.

✒ HOPE FOR THE FUTURE ✒

One of the most memorable Shabbat afternoon gatherings we had in New Haven was in April 2000 when our daughter Hani, on turning twelve years old, was celebrating her *bat mitzvah*. We had flown up about twenty of her classmates from the Jewish day school she attended in Washington to celebrate with us at the Westville Synagogue, placing them at different Shabbat group homes for the weekend. On Saturday afternoon, Hadassah and I hosted the Shabbat group, along with everyone who had flown up from DC, in our New Haven home. Hani led a discussion of the Torah reading, and our son Ethan, who is a rabbi, spoke. Everyone crowded into our living room and adjacent dining room, sitting on chairs or on the floor—mostly Jews, but also some Christian friends from New Haven and Washington—sharing, learning, and singing as the sun set. It was a magical time.

At one point, Dr. Jay Katz—a lawyer, psychiatrist, and neighbor, who was a pioneering faculty member at Yale Law School in the use of psychiatry in law—said he wanted to say something to Hani and her friends. He was born in Germany, and his family had escaped the Holocaust in the 1930s. He spoke of the abuses he witnessed and suffered as a young student in Germany, of his horror and heartbreak when he learned of all the Jewish children who had been murdered by the Nazis. After the Holocaust he feared that there would be no Jewish future. But now, looking around our living room at Hani and her friends—proud, educated, Jewish children—and hearing them speak and sing with such faith and devotion, he said he felt hope for the future. When he was a young person in Germany and Nazism was on the rise, he said he could never have dreamed he would live to see a generation like the one he was looking at. As Jay spoke, he cried, and everyone in the room did too. The tears were tears of gratitude and hope—perfect expressions of the mood that characterizes the closing chapter of each Shabbat.

⚘ WHEN SHABBAT COMES TO AN END ⚘

I have customarily but somewhat imprecisely spoken up until now of the Sabbath "day," a period of time we normally define as twenty-four hours. In that case, the Sabbath should end at sundown, which is when it began. If you've seen the movie *The Frisco Kid*, you may remember the scene when the hero is traveling across the American West by horse. The Frisco Kid, played by Gene Wilder, is a kindly but bumbling, young nineteenth century rabbi on assignment from Eastern Europe to lead the Jews of Gold Rush-era San Francisco. When Shabbat comes, he gets off his horse and leads the animal on foot—technically not correct, since leading an animal is as much a forbidden Sabbath labor as riding it. The film, bless its heart, errs again when the Sabbath ends. Wilder's rabbi waits till the sun has just set and then immediately jumps back on his horse. Again, not correct. The Sabbath doesn't end till the heavens have darkened to the point where we can see three medium-sized stars in the sky. This is defined as nightfall.

Depending on the time of year, nightfall comes almost an hour after sunset, which is added to what would otherwise be a mere twenty-four-hour-long Sabbath. We add to the end of Shabbat and also, as you may recall, a bit to the beginning. We start earlier than we might—out of anticipation and longing—and we end later, for the opposite reason.

It turns out, then, that our Sabbath actually lasts about twenty-five hours. In fact, some Orthodox (particularly Hasidic) Jews take this further and hold a post-Shabbat feast, the *Melaveh Malke*, which means "Accompanying the Queen," the Sabbath bride, as she departs. With more Torah teaching, feasting, and singing, this can extend the Sabbath late into Saturday night.

❧ THE EGALITARIAN QUALITY OF SHABBAT ❧

Rabbi Joseph Soloveitchik recalled a beautiful experience from his childhood about our reluctance to let the Sabbath go. When he was growing up in Lithuania, he would attend a little Lubavitch synagogue for the third meal. Those in attendance would extend their meal with songs, songs, and more songs.

At one point, a well-dressed and distinguished looking man turned to young Joseph and asked if he recognized him. The boy admitted he did not. The man introduced himself as Yankel (the Yiddish diminutive for Jacob) the porter, who did menial work around the town. With his Shabbat manner and attire, Yankel was unrecognizable to the boy. That was because on the Sabbath he was not Yankel the Porter, but Yankel the Prince. Yankel was particularly enthusiastic to keep the songs going, for when the Sabbath was over, he would be Yankel the Porter once again.

Long after nightfall, this was still going on. The evening prayer of *Ma'ariv* had yet to be recited in the synagogue before the congregants could or would go home. With a touch of impatience, the boy asked Yankel, "When do we *daven Ma'ariv*?" That is, when will we say the prayer that concludes the Sabbath?

Yankel looked at him, I imagine with a hint of reproach, and asked, "Do you miss weekdays that much?"

The young Soloveitchik realized then that they were not just singing for the sake of singing but to push off the end of Shabbat and the beginning of the work week as long as they could.

Rabbi Irving "Yitz" Greenberg of Riverdale, New York, whom I have long depended on for counsel, tells a related story, not about a poor man like Yankel, but about a rich man. This wealthy Jewish man was walking home from synagogue one Sabbath day when he suddenly became ill, collapsed, and died. On Shabbat, observant Jews do not carry a wallet—so the man had no money and no identification. Since he was in the habit of dressing modestly, nothing about his physical appearance indicated who this man was. A passerby found his body and the police came and took it away. Because he was unidentifiable, the authorities were thinking they might have to bury him in a potter's field, along with other impoverished, homeless, unidentifiable people, when his family discovered what had happened and retrieved the man's body and identity.

The story seems disturbing at first until, as Rabbi Greenberg teaches, you realize that the reason the man could not be identified was because of what in any other context would be a wonderful thing—the egalitarianism of Shabbat. For on that day, the poor man can think himself a prince, and the rich man takes his place as an equal in the company of his fellow Sabbath observers. This puts us in mind of the final redemption of mankind when we will all be equals, undifferentiated by circumstances of birth or fortune, nation or faith that divide us now in this imperfect world.

❧ MAKING DISTINCTIONS AND BRINGING ORDER ☙

When the twenty-five hours of Sabbath have ended, then the evening services, *Ma'ariv* and *Havdalah*, can be said.

In the synagogue in Stamford, at this point we leave the social hall and return to the sanctuary. At home in Washington, we go to the living room. The evening service contains most of the same prayers said in every weekday evening service—the *Borchu* call to prayer; the *Shema* declaration of faith; and once again, the standing, silent *Amidah*—with a few additions appropriate to the end of Shabbat.

Now we are truly at the end of the Sabbath, and the new week is about to begin. It is a time of transition, and distinction. The words added to the *Amidah* of Saturday evening make that point and broaden it powerfully beyond the separation between Shabbat and the six days to other distinctions we humans are uniquely capable of making. This is because God gave us free will, the ability to distinguish and to bring order out of chaos. In that way we come to be God's partners in Creation. The words added are:

You have graced us with the knowledge of Your Torah, and taught us to perform the statutes of Your will. You have distinguished, Lord our God, between the holy and the secular, light and darkness, Israel and the nations, and between the seventh day and the six days of labor. Our Father, our King, may the days approaching us bring peace; may we be free from all sin, cleansed from all iniquity, holding fast to our reverence of You.

These words of distinction will soon be echoed in the ceremony of *Havdalah*, which literally means "distinction." Of all the blessings in the *Amidah* in which the rabbis could have placed those additional words, they chose to do so in the prayer for knowledge, insight, and wisdom, and their reason is clear and important. The Jerusalem Talmud (*Berachot* 5:2) asks, "If there is no knowledge, how can there be distinctions?" In other words, without the miraculous capacities God put into the human mind, we would not be able to make the distinctions and choices we need to make to love and serve God. Our mind is the most God-like of all our human qualities. God gave us the ability to understand the dynamics of the solar system. God gave us the capacity to decipher the sequence of DNA, the code of life. We were meant to use these talents to join with God in improving and perfecting the world. Most of all we are called to use our mind to understand the difference between good and evil and to choose good.

❧ THE *HAVDALAH* CEREMONY ❧

At the end of the evening service, it is time for *Havdalah*, a ceremony that is rich in reassuring rituals, symbols, and another call for insight and good judgment. Wine is poured to overflowing in a silver cup held by the person reciting the prayers. A braided candle with at least two wicks is lit and held by another person. It is the first fire we have created since the Sabbath began on Friday and a clear statement that the Sabbath is over. A box, usually also silver, containing a mixture of fragrant spices is brought to the table where *Havdalah* is being said.

I believe *Havdalah* can be a unique unifier of those who observe Sabbath and those who do not. It is accessible to Jews of all denominations, as well as to non-Jews. For many people the lights, wine, and spices are easier to access than the formal liturgy of services. To some, it may seem inconsistent to celebrate the ceremony concluding Shabbat if you have not observed Shabbat itself, but I think it can be a comfortable door into Shabbat for many people, even though strictly speaking it is the door *out* of Shabbat.

Some years ago, Hadassah and I were asked to speak at a convention of the Young Leadership of the Jewish Federations of North America at a resort outside Phoenix. There were prayer services on Saturday morning, divided by denominations—Reform, Conservative, and Orthodox. The attendance for these services was small. Yet when Shabbat was over, *everyone* gathered for *Havdalah*, outside in the open air, in a very uplifting and unifying service. I know that some of the most successful and attractive Jewish outreach centers have made use of this unique quality of *Havdalah*. Hadassah and I have attended really spiritual *bar* and *bat mitzvahs* celebrated in synagogues directly after the *Havdalah* services. As Shabbat ends, a Saturday-night reception begins. For years, the famous Brandeis-Bardin Institute in Southern California has held a beautifully choreographed *Havdalah* as the climax of its Sabbath celebrations, drawing Jews from all backgrounds to the dramatically situated, rugged campus of the institute. Many Jews from the Los Angeles area who were inspired to reconnect to their Jewish heritage trace their spiritual journey back to the influence of Brandeis-Bardin with its Shabbat-ending *Havdalah* service.

At one level, the ritual of *Havdalah* serves the same purpose that *Kiddush* did at the inauguration of the Sabbath. Because the Sabbath is so special and different from the days that precede and follow it, we need to decisively mark it off from the rest of the week both at the beginning and at the end. There are three elements of *Havdalah* that make it so captivating:

WINE

Just as we said *Kiddush* on Friday night over wine, we do the same at *Havdalah*. The medieval Spanish sage Maimonides held that fulfilling the biblical commandment to "Remember the Sabbath Day" requires not just acts but words. So, with one person holding the candle, another person who is holding the wine cup, recites a paragraph of reassuring prayers from the Prophets and Psalms.

Then the leader raises the cup of wine and says *Havdalah*.

Rabbi "Yitz" Greenberg teaches that just as the *Kiddush* on Friday night sanctifies the Sabbath, *Havdalah* on Saturday night sanctifies the days of work ahead. We pour the wine so

that it overflows the lip of the cup as a sign of our hope that
God will cause His blessings and goodness to overflow in our
lives during the week ahead.

SPICES

Then, the spice box is picked up, the blessing thanking God
for creating fragrant spices is said, and spices are passed around
the room so that everyone can smell (or, as my family says of
me, inhale) the aroma.

Earlier I described the Jewish belief that when the Sabbath
comes, we are blessed with an additional soul. I think of it as an
extra dimension of spirituality. Sadly, when the Sabbath ends,
this extra soul returns to God and we feel a sense of loss. Some
say the spices are inhaled to revive our spirits.

A similar explanation for the spices I have heard is that they
allow us to leave the Sabbath, Shabbatland, with their sweet
smell in our nostrils. We can then take that wonderful sensual, hope-filled memory with us throughout the week, until
the next Sabbath comes.

This reminds me of a brief personal story. As I've mentioned, I lost a campaign for Congress in 1980. At the Sabbath services on the following Saturday, the Torah portion
of the week happened to be the story from Genesis of Joseph
being sold into slavery by his brothers. The buyers were spice
merchants who took Joseph to Egypt. Jacob Mendelson, who
was my rabbi then, said the spices were a gift from God to
Joseph so that although he had been so unfairly abused by his
brothers, the sweet smell of the spices would accompany him
on his forced journey to Egypt to give him hope that there
were better times ahead for him. The rabbi noted my election loss and said he hoped I could smell similar spices and

go forward on my personal journey with optimism. It was a lovely, uplifting message, which I often think about when I inhale the spices at the beginning of the new week's journey from Shabbat.

LIGHT

Finally, the braided candle with at least two wicks is held up, and a blessing that acknowledges God as the Creator of the lights of fire is said. The multiple wicks of the *Havdalah* candle are meant to represent not just light but the power of fire. Fire is the primordial human creation that powers civilization. Fire cooks food, making it edible; fire gives heat, freeing people from vulnerability and dependency on nature. We celebrate this human power because it enables us to join as partners with God in upgrading the world. Since this is the first creative act of the new week, the blessing is the first blessing of the new week. We hold our hands out to the flame with our palms up and bend our fingers inward to create a shadow across our palms. Some say that is to show that not only is this the first fire we have created since sunset on Friday, but to see the shadow across our hands, which is the first product of the first creative act of the new week. Others say we do this because it will be through our hands that we interact with the world in the six days of labor ahead. Through the creativity of our hands, we try to uplift the world. Both of those interpretations have meaning to me, as does the most obvious: light gives us hope at the beginning of the week, particularly a week that begins in the darkness of Saturday night.

The braided candle recalls the very first Sabbath of creation—which, according to tradition, Adam and Eve were allowed by God to spend in the Garden of Eden, even after the primordial sin. On Saturday afternoon, when they saw the sun begin to set, they knew that they would soon be banished to the imperfect world outside of Eden. Adam feared the darkness and the terror it contains, but God in His kindness gave Adam a great gift. He showed him how to make fire—a creative act that formed the template of all human creativity that would come thereafter, and again enabled man to create and distinguish and begin the long journey back to Eden. As Rabbi Sacks writes:

> Shabbat is our weekly return to the harmony and serenity of the Garden of Eden. As the day ends, we, like Adam and Eve, prepare to reengage with the world—a world often fraught with dangers. We pray to God to be with us in the days ahead, to protect us from harm, and to bless the work of our hands.

❧ THE IMPORTANCE OF MAKING DISTINCTIONS ❧

In concluding *Havdalah*, we recite the formal blessing of separation itself:

> Blessed are You, Lord our God, King of the Universe, who separates between holy and secular, between light and darkness, between Israel and the nations, between the seventh day and the six days of labor. Blessed are You, Lord, who separates between holy and secular.

In this prayer, we thank God for the distinctions He has made and the capacity he has given us to see those distinctions. *Havdalah* is not a ceremony that divides all the world into a simple dichotomy of good and evil, saved and damned, clean and unclean. The text of the final *Havdalah* blessing is clearly not making a separation based on right and wrong, since there is nothing wrong with the six days of labor (which are commanded in the Torah) or the nations of the world (who are all God's children) or darkness (which is the natural result of God's creation of the earth and the way it turns in relationship to the sun) or the secular (which does not mean evil). In some ways the *Havdalah* blessing asks us to bring these categories together—to fill darkness with light, to sanctify the secular. In other ways, separation really means making distinctions—not dividing areas and people into categories but rather appreciating the variety and distinctiveness of cultures, faiths, and lifestyles. Without these separations, life would be much less interesting, the free will God gave us would have no space in which to make choices, and our earthly mission to perfect this world would be hollow.

The faith that I have been given and taught is all about seeing and making clear and proper distinctions and choices. Sometimes that means we have to say no—or to pass on something appealing because of a higher commitment or fundamental purpose. The Law revealed on Mt. Sinai was, as has often been said, not Ten Suggestions, but Ten Commandments. God made some big choices, and so of course must we. In the Talmud the rabbis interpret and apply these choices in page after page of careful and sometimes minute gradations and distinctions. For example, in the Talmud's first book, *Berachot* ("Blessings"), there is a section on the time at which morning prayers may begin, which includes an extended discussion of the quality of light that differentiates the transition from before dawn to dawn. This kind of inquiry is important and helps us understand the levels of goodness, degrees of error, and the value of taking partial steps toward large goals.

Havdalah therefore impresses on us the imperative to use our intellect to distinguish things from one another. The timing of that lesson could not be better, because as the Sabbath ends, we are about to leave Shabbatland and return to the world with all its temptations—selfishness, thoughtlessness, anger, greed, and lust. We need the knowledge and strength that comes from God to discipline ourselves and help us make the right choices. But choose we must, no matter how difficult those choices may be.

This life view is antithetical to moral relativism, which rejects the separations entailed by moral distinctions. In a relativist framework, moral distinctions and choices are an illusion we foist on an otherwise meaningless and purely physical existence. Of course, I don't see things that way. And for me, the Sabbath and *Havdalah* serve as a recurring reminder of the need to distinguish and decide.

The fact is that life continually confronts us with choices, and many of them are moral choices. I learned this early on from my parents, who were very deliberate in crafting the moral outlook they taught me and my sisters. To call our parents either "permissive" or "strict" would miss the point. They clearly decided in which areas they would be permissive and in which they would be strict. For example, my sisters Rietta, Ellen, and I did not have bedtimes. Even as little children, we were permitted to stay up until we fell asleep—sometimes not even in our beds but on the floor. In other areas—such as religious observance, performance at school, and personal behavior—my parents held us firmly accountable. And they were very good at guilt induction. My father was not a man who yelled a lot, but he could rebuke and motivate with a few quiet, well-placed, words and an angry or disappointed face. He knew how to teach my sisters and me to make distinctions.

One story, which may seem irrelevant and certainly old-fashioned, comes to mind as an example of Mom and Dad's parenting. During high school, my friends and I slipped into a bad pattern of driving into New York and drinking on Saturday nights. One night, I had much too much, and one of my friends had to help me into the house. He deposited me in the first floor half-bathroom where I proceeded to vomit excessively and loudly. My mother found me there and pulled me upstairs to get cleaned up. I remember her crying, "You have ruined your life." At the top of the stairs, I could see my sisters, awakened and now also crying, apparently worried that I had murdered someone. The next morning, I got up with a terrible hangover. The room was spinning wildly around me. My dad came in, and his eyes cut through me with disappointment and disdain. He sternly and simply said, "You should have known that what you were doing was wrong and dangerous. Don't ever do that again." I didn't.

My father and mother were very ethical people. With their example and the teachings of my faith, including the lessons of each Sabbath, I have tried throughout my life to make moral distinctions and right decisions. I know I have not always seen the distinctions clearly or made the decisions correctly. But I keep trying.

When I was elected to office and, therefore, became a public figure, I knew from my religious learning that the standards applied to my behavior would now be higher because the consequences of my misbehavior as a public person would be greater. The Bible clearly teaches the lesson that the most powerful are not above the law but more intensely subjected to it. The most poignant example of this rule is God's refusal to allow Moses to enter the Holy Land, notwithstanding all his righteous leadership, because he lost his temper and/or confidence and, to pacify the angry Israelites, struck the rock at Marah to produce water instead of speaking to the rock as God had instructed him.

When I became Connecticut's attorney general, I remember saying to my staff, "We are going to have a rule of behavior in this office that I will call 'The Front Page Rule.' I will assume that none of us will ever do anything that is illegal or unethical. But I want to go a step further. I want to make sure that we will never do anything that we cannot explain and justify if we are criticized for it on the front page of any newspaper." (That, as you can see, was prior to the coming of cable news and internet bloggers.)

As a senator, I constantly have to make decisions when I vote. There are only two real choices: "aye" or "no." One of the hardest public choices I have ever had to make was not on a legislative vote but on the questions of what to do when it became clear in 1998 that President Clinton had an immoral relationship with a young woman named Monica Lewinsky.

I had known Bill Clinton since 1970 when he was at Yale Law School. He volunteered that year in my first state senate campaign. He and I kept in touch over the years, and both developed the same ideology as centrist Democrats. I was an early supporter of his presidential campaign in 1992 and was proud of so much that he had accomplished. But the behavior with Lewinsky, which he finally acknowledged in a televised address in August of 1998, was disgraceful. I was deeply troubled that President Clinton had refused to take real responsibility for his unacceptable behavior. I knew it was not only wrong but, because he was president, would have terrible consequences throughout our country. In Congress, the reaction to this matter reflexively divided along party lines, even though there was nothing ideological or partisan about what Clinton and Lewinsky had done. Republicans attacked Clinton. Democrats defended him or maintained an awkward silence. Some argued that we Americans should show the maturity of the Europeans and look aside when our leaders indulged themselves. That was classic moral relativism, which I rejected.

In the midst of this growing crisis, I received a call from the conservative thinker and activist Bill Bennett, with whom I had been working to combat the impact on our children of sex and violence in the media. Bill talked about the relationship of that work to what Clinton had done and urged me to think about the example of the prophet Nathan, who chastised King David for his affair with Bathsheba and for arranging the death of her husband.

"Bill," I said, "I'm a senator, not a prophet."

"I know," he answered, "but you are a senator who knows right from wrong, and your country needs someone like you to say that what the president has done is very wrong."

In Connecticut, during that August, people kept stopping me—on the street, in the supermarket, even on the beach—asking me what I thought about Clinton's behavior and what I was going to do about it. I remember one woman who pleaded with me: "You of all people must speak out because you have been so strong in opposing the terrible influence of TV, movies, and other media on our children. Now, because of Clinton, my young children are asking me about oral sex. This is outrageous."

Hadassah and I had rented a house near the beach in Madison, Connecticut, for a week that month for the whole family. Around the Shabbat table in that house, we talked about Clinton and Lewinsky. The generational responses were a surprise to me. The children were of one mind. They argued that I should say what I and they believed—that Clinton's behavior was immoral and that he must accept responsibility and apologize for it. Hadassah was torn. My mom was Clinton's lone defender. She loved him and thought that even though he had made a mistake, he should be forgiven for it, and I should remain silent.

In the end, I decided I had to speak out.

On September 4, 1998, I went to the Senate floor and condemned the president's behavior as "immoral, harmful" and "too consequential for us to walk away from." I was the first prominent Democrat to do so, and my speech received much greater attention than I expected. Rejecting the president's argument that his relationship with Ms. Lewinsky was "nobody's business" but his family's and his claim that "even presidents have private lives," I said: "Whether he or we think it is fair or not—the reality is that a president's private life is public." When a president acts badly, I argued, even in private, he risks gravely damaging our country and compromising the trust of the people he was elected to serve and lead.

A week later, the president convened an extraordinary interfaith group of clergy men and women at the White House and publicly apologized for his behavior. He asked them to pray with him as he worked to repair the damage he had done. On the following Sunday morning, I was at home in Washington. It was around 9:30 when the White House operator called and said she had President Clinton on the line. He and I had a long, largely religious conversation between two old friends, in which he said how much he regretted his behavior, told me he understood why I made the speech I did, and said he was meeting regularly with two ministers to get himself and his family back on track.

I thanked the president and told him I knew, as a matter of personal experience and faith, that every one of us is imperfect and depends on God's mercy and forgiveness and that of our fellow humans to keep us going.

I don't know whether President Clinton went to church later that Sunday morning, but I felt that in our long phone conversation, he and I had had a deeply religious, Sabbath experience.

And, incidentally, I voted against President Clinton's impeachment, making another choice and distinction, this one based on my conclusion that the president's personal behavior did not constitute an impeachable offense as contemplated by the Framers of our Constitution.

Someone once said to me that Bill Clinton is like everyone else except more so. In fact, his life has been a most prominent example of the human condition: imperfect but capable of genuine goodness and real greatness. As the Sabbath ends each week, we pray for the promised redemption, knowing that our world remains broken but fixable and that we remain imperfect but perfectible. The choices are ours. *Havdalah* reminds us of all that.

After the last *Havdalah* blessing is said, the candle is either blown out or doused in the wine. The electric lights go on, and we sing a farewell to the Sabbath, "May He who distinguishes between sacred and secular forgive our sins."

And finally, we sing a song of tribute and calling to Elijah the Prophet, who we believe will herald the coming of the Messiah. As the prophet Malachi wrote: "Behold, I will send you Elijah, the prophet, before the coming of the great and dreadful day of the Lord" (3:23).

Over the years, I have learned and felt two reasons for this calling out to Elijah at the beginning of the new week. First, it expresses our hope that Elijah and the Messiah will come in the week ahead; and second, it is our statement of resolve to live and act in a way during the new week that will, step by step, hasten the coming of the Messiah.

So, as we leave the synagogue, we wish each other "*Shavua tov!*" "A good week!" It is a greeting that means what it says but implies a lot more. We are rested and ready to go back to work until the Sabbath comes again next Friday.

But I don't want to leave you with the impression that after we depart from the synagogue on Saturday evening, it closes until nightfall on the following Friday. In fact, the synagogue is open every day, with morning, afternoon, and evening prayer services and a lot of educational and social activities too. I am sure there is a special place in Heaven for the people who keep those services and activities going every weekday until the rest of the community returns to synagogue on the Sabbath.

❧ SIMPLE BEGINNINGS ❧

❧ The close of Sabbath is the ideal time to think about the brokenness of our world and to long and pray for its redemption.

❧ Have a light evening meal with family as the Sabbath draws to a close. Depending on the time of year, this may mean an early or a later dinner. Feel the tinge of sadness that comes with the day's departure.

❧ Read or sing Psalm 23, which offers God's assurance of His providential protection as we contemplate the coming week.

❧ If you had an opportunity to study Scripture during the Sabbath, review what you learned and talk about it with a friend or family member.

❧ Consider celebrating a version of *Havdalah* in your home—with candles, wine, and spices—as a way to separate from your Sabbath rest and prepare yourself to reenter your workweek.

❧ Chapter Ten ❧

THE SIX DAYS OF LABOR:

WORKING WITH A PURPOSE

W e've spent the preceding nine chapters experiencing the Sabbath together, carrying out the fourth commandment that God gave to Moses and mankind. But I don't want all I have said about the beauty of Sabbath rest to mislead you into thinking that the fourth commandment is only about resting.

Let's look at the text again: "Six days shalt thou labor and do all thy work: but the seventh day is a Sabbath to the Lord, your God: in it thou shalt not do any work" (Exodus 20:9–10). As you can see, there are actually two commanded activities here, not one. The second is to rest on the seventh day. But the first is to work—to "labor and do all thy work"—on the other six days of the week. The fourth commandment is no less serious about the one (work) than the other (rest).

In this chapter, I want to describe the ways that biblical tradition urges us to experience not only our rest but also our work as commandments and gifts from God. The Sabbath receives its meaning from the six days in which we labor, as our workdays receive their meaning from the rest we enjoy on the Sabbath. Each is dependent on the other. Each enriches the other.

When the Sabbath ends, we are sent out once again into God's world to "till it and to keep it" (Genesis 2:15). To survive in God's world, work is necessary, as the first "hunters and gatherers" found out and as each of us still knows today. The first thing I do after the Sabbath is go directly to my BlackBerry and read the messages that have come in. God created this miraculous world for humans, but if our ancestors had just rested and waited for food and shelter to come along, human history would have been very short. They had to work to live, even in the Garden of Eden. If you believe, as I do, that God created us not only to enjoy His world but to improve and ultimately perfect it, then that surely requires hard work. Through our labor on the six days, we strive to imitate and serve God, and then on the Sabbath—like God—we rest and hallow the day. Work and rest together form an organic whole, in a mutually reinforcing relationship.

☙ PHYSICAL STAMINA ❧

Putting rest into our week gives us extra energy to do the work that improves our lives and gives us satisfaction. I certainly find this to be so. I have always been able to work harder on the six days knowing that the seventh day of rest is coming.

When young people interested in a political career ask me what qualities a person most needs in order to succeed at running for and keeping public office, I say: "Of course, you should be well informed about the issues. You should know how to think and how to learn. You should be able to communicate and cooperate effectively with other people. You need self-confidence and the ability to respond quickly on your feet to questions and challenges. But none of those endowments will take you as far as you want to go in the political world if you don't also have a lot of of sheer physical stamina. I know that I could not have done the things I have in public life if I had not been taught by my parents the importance and pleasure of good, hard work."

My mother began working in a bakery when she was twelve. As you may remember, her father, Joseph, for whom I was named, died when he was young, so my grandmother, Baba, was left a widow with five children. They all needed to go to work as soon as they could. Mom worked until she married Dad and I was born, but at busy times of the year she joined him at the liquor store, and when he went into the U.S. Army in World War II, she ran the store for almost two years. My memories of Mom are of a woman in motion—inside the house, cleaning and cooking; outside, shopping (her favorite) or volunteering in community organizations, from our synagogue's bingo night to the public library's used-book store. She continued in motion pretty much until her death at age ninety. "I will walk as long as I can walk," Mom said to me later in her life. "When I need a walker, I will use it to get around. And then if I need to crawl to go to where I want to go, I will crawl." That was Mom.

My father was a man of average size and extraordinary strength. He worked long and hard, without complaining, whether it was at his first job on an overnight bakery truck; or lifting cases of beer and liquor in his store; or painting, wallpapering, or gardening at his house or his children's houses. He never complained about doing physical labor but seemed to draw satisfaction from it because he knew it was his path to accomplishment.

Mom and Dad would tell my sisters and me, "There will be plenty of time to rest in the next world. So in this world, work as hard as you can and enjoy it as much as you can." That is a perfect summary of the fourth commandment, isn't it?

My father's example also encouraged me to stay in good physical condition. Every day, Pop would do what he called "calisthenics" and we now call "stretching" exercises. He bowled with a team, was a very strong swimmer and skater, and when he retired, he walked more than five miles most days. More than I expected, the ability to work long and hard has mattered in my career. Serving in public office and running a political campaign—especially if at the same time—is a real challenge. It is tough to do without getting exhausted, which raises the risk of making a mistake that can cost you dearly. My vice presidential campaign in 2000 was probably the most grueling of my career because it went all across this big country of ours.

In 2000, I typically worked at least eighteen hour days and could only look forward to four to six hours of sleep at night, if I was lucky. In the weeks before the vice presidential debate with Dick Cheney, my schedule was very demanding. Our son Matt was with us in the last few days of preparation for the debate in Danville, Kentucky. At one point he told Hadassah he was worried about me. He'd never seen me so tired. "The light's gone out of his eyes," Matt told Hadassah. "His brain is all there, but his soul isn't coming through." She repeated that to me. It jolted me from my fatigue, and I think, reconnected me to my soul. The family was with me backstage before that debate and I said, "Let's sing something to get me in the right mood going out there." Matt has a strong baritone voice and he began to sing, "This little light of mine, I'm going to let it shine." The whole family joined in and I was ready.

During the 2000 race, I experienced the most dramatic contrasts between the Sabbath and the start of my work week. Saturday night after sunset was almost always extremely busy. As soon as we'd finished with *Havdalah*, there'd be a fund-raiser wherever I had spent Shabbat, or I'd jump on a plane to travel to wherever my schedule would begin on Sunday morning, or there would be staff briefings to prepare for a Sunday morning TV show or to map out the week ahead. When I was lucky enough to spend Shabbat at home, Saturday night was a time to take care of personal needs, like getting a haircut from my Washington barber, Renato Stalteri, who was kind enough to come over to our home after dark to cut my hair.

We spent the last Sabbath of the 2000 campaign in South Florida. The state was a very clearly and hotly contested battle ground, on whose vote, as it happened, the ultimate outcome of the race would hinge. I had campaigned there as close to sunset on that last Friday as I could. Because I knew what was coming after darkness fell on Saturday, I enjoyed a very satisfying Shabbat afternoon nap. Then after *Havdalah*, Hadassah and I began a circuit of our entire country, which kept us traveling from Saturday night through Tuesday night when the polls closed, a total of seventy-two hours during which I probably got twelve hours of sleep. The first stop after Shabbat was Miami's Little Havana where I had two cups of very strong, sweet Cuban coffee which, I am sure, helped me get by with so little sleep during the following three days. From there I went up to Central Florida, over to New Mexico and

Nevada, up to Oregon and Washington, over to Wisconsin, Minnesota, Maine, and New Hampshire, down to Pennsylvania and then on Tuesday, to Tampa, Florida—where I joined Al Gore for a sunrise rally—after which I flew up to New Haven to vote and then down to Nashville for last minute TV and radio and election returns.

My parents' example and the certainty of the Sabbath coming every seventh day enabled me to run that course and a lot of others and still be on my feet.

Insights Gained in Quiet Times

The Sabbath also helps us work better in other, less physical and obvious ways. Rabbi Daniel Lapin of Seattle writes in his very interesting book, *Thou Shall Prosper,* about the Torah's lessons for success in work and business. He has an important insight about the advantage that comes from being able to set aside quiet time on Shabbat to think about and discern patterns in your personal life and in your career. Whoever we are and whatever we do, stepping back from the noise and confusion of the daily hustle to gain a broader perspective is valuable.

Quiet times are the best for this. I know that some of my best ideas come when I've managed to tune out the distractions of life. Rabbi Lapin points out that in a quiet, dark house at night, you hear things you never hear during the day—like the sound of the refrigerator cycling on and off. The Sabbath is a quiet, dark house where we suddenly notice things—trends in the world around us and ideas that pop into our heads out of nowhere and would be overlooked during the week.

❧ EARNING WEALTH AS
A WORTHY CALLING ❧

Mark Twain once observed that Jews seem to have a gift for work and business. Part of the reason, Rabbi Lapin believes, is that the Torah regards earning a living as a worthy calling. We naturally do better in endeavors that we feel to be worthy than in ones we dismiss as lacking value. The Mishnah says in its tractate *Pirkei Avot* ("Ethics of the Fathers") that the world stands on three fundamental virtues. According to the sage and high priest Simon the Just, who lived around 300 B.C. those three virtues are learning the Torah, praying, and doing acts of kindliness. The word that Simon used for praying, *avodah*, means both the worship service in the Temple and work in the sense of creative activity. In fact, the rabbis of the Talmud and Midrash saw honest and ethical work as a form of service to others, since we make money if we satisfy our fellow human beings by providing a service or product they need or want.

Remember that when we observe the Sabbath, we are affirming and honoring God's design and creation of the world, which were surely the greatest acts of investment, innovation, and productivity ever. Maybe that's one reason biblical tradition does not display the ambivalence toward wealth that we often find in our contemporary culture. It sees work done to produce wealth—so long as honestly achieved—as a positive act through which we serve God's purpose for us and, incidentally, provide ourselves with the resources to care for other people in need.

To some people it may seem improper for spiritual leaders to praise the attainment of wealth—or to work to become wealthy. They seem to believe that clergy men and women should be untainted by work and wealth-creation. Yet interestingly, in the Jewish context the idea of a full-time professional rabbinate goes back only as far as the Middle Ages. Before that, rabbis rolled up their sleeves and got their hands dirty. The greatest rabbis of the medieval period all had jobs and careers. The eleventh century French scholar Rashi, whose commentaries on the Bible and Talmud are still the standard, was a wine maker. Maimonides and Nachmanides, the great twelfth and thirteenth century Spanish sages, were both physicians. In earlier epochs, some of the most distinguished rabbinic sages did manual labor and were skilled in crafts. Even in more modern times, we find that a revered rabbinic figure like the Chofetz Chaim (1838–1933), who authored a beloved commentary on the Code of Jewish Law, ran a grocery store with his wife.

One of the classical rabbinic philosophers, the Spanish sage Bachya ben Joseph ibn Paquda, wrote a guide to Jewish faith and practice called *The Duties of the Heart*, in which he argues that God provides for us in every way, including the way he inspires each of us with a passion for a particular field of work to the exclusion of other fields. More recently, Rabbi Menachem Schneerson taught that the work we do is a way that God actually chooses for us to be His emissary to the world. We're not just earning a living. We are, to quote the Blues Brothers, "on a mission from God" to do the best job we can in our career and to serve other people through our work as well as we are able. I think my father had something like this in mind when he once responded to my frustration that a man of his obvious intellect never had the opportunity to have a professional career: "Maybe that's not what I was meant to do," he said.

❧ Seeing Work as Your Mission ❧

In the movie *Jerry Maguire*, Tom Cruise plays a high-powered sports agent who's in the work strictly for the money: "Show me the money!" as Jerry's client, played by Cuba Gooding, Jr., famously demands of him. By the end, after realizing there's more to work than making money, Jerry reenvisions his career not as a job but as a *mission*. It was the same job, but he came to see it differently. He gave it meaning.

For many people, probably most people, the meaning of their work, their mission, is providing for their family. And, when you think about it, what could be more important than working to be able to pay for what your family needs to live and what your children need to flourish. That has been the great mission of generations of immigrants to America. It has been and continues to be their American Dream. They work hard to succeed, and, if they don't go as far as they might wish, then they work to make sure their children do.

My father taught me this lesson in a conversation he and Mom and I had after he retired. I told them that someone I knew had just moved into a big house up the hill from where his liquor store had been. They both said they knew exactly which house it was. "Let me tell you a story about that house and your father," Mom said. "When he first opened the store, he actually walked from house to house in the neighborhood to introduce himself and his store and ask for business. When he came to that big house, which was occupied by a very wealthy family, whoever answered the door said they had a dirty basement and if he would clean it up for nothing, they would probably give him their liquor business. Well, Joseph, I can tell you, your father worked for a day and a half to clean that basement.

It was filthy. I remember Dad telling me he found dead mice and all sorts of junk and grease there. But he got it done, and those people bought all their liquor from him from then on."

I looked at my father and said, "Dad, I've got to tell you, it makes me angry that those people forced you to clean their basement without paying you in order to get their liquor business."

But my dad said, "Don't be angry Joseph, I wasn't angry. I was starting the business and I had very few customers. I had a wife to support, and we wanted to have children. So I did what I had to do, and that family bought a lot of liquor from me for years after that. And of course, what I was able to make from the liquor store, I used to buy this house and do a lot of other things, including paying for college and graduate school for you, Rietta, and Ellen. So, cleaning the basement was worth it."

From my father's great insight and the Bible's wisdom, I have come to understand the deeper meaning of work and rest. I believe that all of creation bears the stamp of God's creative intentions, down to the most microscopic elements of nature and human life. Just as no detail of God's work of creation was too small to attract His interest because it was all important, so too, no detail of the work each one of us does is without significance and meaning. In our work we each contribute to the whole; we each continue God's work of creation.

❧ WORK—A PARTNERSHIP WITH GOD ☙

At Friday's dinner and Saturday's lunch before we enjoyed the delicious *challah*, we thanked God for "bringing forth bread from the earth." Of course it's not literally true that loaves of bread spring from the ground. You can't find a loaf of *challah* bread hanging on a stalk of wheat. Wheat and water, the ingredients of bread, come respectively from the earth and sky. For wheat to become *challah* requires the coordinated and creative efforts of human beings working together—growing and harvesting the wheat, making it into flour, mixing it with other ingredients, kneading it, baking, packaging, and distributing it. So we praise God for blessing us with the ability to cooperate with His creation and with other people that makes possible the production of bread from the earth and grain that God has given us. The same is true of how olives become oil and grapes become wine. I mention grain, oil, and wine because these are the specific rewards promised to us (in Deuteronomy 11:14) if we love the Lord our God and serve Him with all our heart and soul. To enjoy the reward, however, we must work. We must take God's creation, and with our own creativity, make it into something that sustains and improves our lives. When we work, we become God's active partners in improving the world until we perfect it. There is great challenge, excitement, and joy in such work.

That's why I believe that the Sabbath is a covenant and so, too, is our work a partnership with the Holy One. Both the Sabbath and work are commandments and gifts from God— each reinforcing the other. The Sabbath and the six days of labor together give us the greatest gifts of all: the gifts of meaning, purpose, and destiny. Rest without work would be meaningless. Work without rest would be purposeless. But together, work and rest offer us the hope of a better life today and the destiny of ultimate redemption tomorrow.

❧ SIMPLE BEGINNINGS ❧

❧ Ask yourself: what mission are you fulfilling in your daily work? In what ways can you consider your job or your volunteer work an act of service or worship, whether to God or other human beings?

❧ If you turned off your computer, cell phone, and/ or TV for the Sabbath—which is my number one Simple Beginnings suggestion to you—as you now prepare to power them up again, think about the fact that you can get by without them! Remember the feeling of liberation that came with seeing them go dark. Consider minimizing the place of electronic media in your life and the life of your family. Encourage your children to read books and play outside rather than crouch before a computer game. Consider setting a "bedtime" for your computer and TV each night: After this hour, the machines are turned off and not turned on again till the next day.

❧ On the Sabbath, be attuned to the meaning and messages about life that, on a busy workday, you would otherwise likely miss. In the coming week, how can you incorporate or profit from what you learned on the Sabbath?

- Consider how, in your work, you do and can act as God's partner in creation.

- Start planning ahead now for the next Sabbath. Count the days till it comes!

MAKING YOUR OWN SABBATH

We live in a culture of hard work where people are desperately in need of rest—not just rest to recharge our batteries so we can work harder but to recharge our souls so we can live better. For me, the answer to that need has been the Sabbath. It has anchored my life, revived my body, and restored my soul. I know the Sabbath can do the same for you.

In this book, we have experienced a traditional Jewish Sabbath together with all its rituals, rules, and customs. As we have discussed, Jewish Sabbath laws were transmitted by rabbis over the centuries to implement the broad commandment in the Bible to honor the Sabbath. The rabbis made clear that they were building a fence around the Torah and the Sabbath to assure that both would be protected and upheld. It was this form of Sabbath observance that I was born into, and through it, I have found pleasure, purpose, and community.

But the traditional Jewish way is not the only way to observe and enjoy the Sabbath. No matter what your faith or how religious you are or are not, you can find your own way to bring the Sabbath—God's gift of rest—into your life. And, remember, it doesn't have to be all or nothing.

Years ago, I knew a wonderful man in New Haven named Arthur Spiegel who once neatly summarized my concluding appeal to you. Arthur was executive director of the local Jewish Federation and a gregarious and cultured man. He loved the Sabbath and regularly attended Sabbath services but did not observe every point of Jewish law. He "made Shabbat" in his own way. Once Arthur and I were talking about a mutual friend, a good man, who often went to synagogue on Saturday morning and then to lunch at a restaurant, followed by a movie—both activities that traditional observance forbids. "You know, Joe," Arthur said to me, "Everyone can make their own Shabbat."

That is a profound and important thought. Different people find different ways to "remember the Sabbath day" and, in their own way—even if not exactly in the Talmud's prescribed way—to "keep it holy."

At the end of every chapter in this book, I have suggested steps you can take to get started enjoying the Sabbath. And at the end of the book, you will find several books listed that will tell you more about the Sabbath than I have been able to tell you here. Your Sabbath rest may be on Sunday or Friday rather than Saturday, and it may not include going to a house of worship. In any case, I hope that the first step you take will only be the beginning of your observance and that it will grow from there. But, if you simply decide to go to your chosen house of worship on your Sabbath, or turn off your computer or your television that day, or bless your children, or forgo shopping, or enjoy a family meal, then I will rejoice for you and your family will rejoice as well.

I have learned much from the philosophy of the Lubavitch Hasidic movement, whose rebbe, Menachem Mendel

Schneerson, emphasized the importance of not chastising nonobservant Jews for the commandments they were not doing. Instead, Rabbi Schneerson asked his emissaries to work to convince the nonobservant to do one more good deed or observe one more commandment, like lighting the Sabbath candles, or saying the prayer of thanks before eating bread, or contributing more to charity. Often, as Rabbi Schneerson knew, one religious observance leads to another, and the ultimate effect on the individual and the world can be truly great.

The Talmud contains a wonderful teaching that if everyone observed two Sabbaths in a row, the Messiah would come and preside over the redemption of humanity. On the surface, this vision seems inconsistent with other Talmudic teachings that the appearance of the Messiah will be totally unexpected, perhaps even unrecognized at first. So what did the rabbis mean when they said that two globally observed Sabbaths would bring in the Messianic Age? I think they were saying that the Sabbath has the power to mend the breach that separates human beings from each other and from God, and that closing those two breaches will create the conditions for redemption.

If all of us would just stop and observe one Sabbath and then another in perfect unity with God and one another, then the world would be redeemed.

Until then, each day of Sabbath rest that you choose to observe will give you a taste of the World to Come. The Sabbath is truly a gift. A gift from God. The gift of rest. I hope and pray that you will accept it and let Sabbath rest enrich your life.

ACKNOWLEDGMENTS

The idea of writing this book emerged first in conversations I had with my friend Rabbi Menachem Genack, CEO and rabbinic administrator of the Orthodox Union's kosher food division and a gifted teacher with whom I have studied for years. Rabbi Genack was persistent in his encouragement of the project, even connecting me with my collaborator, David Klinghoffer, whom I had known slightly as the literary editor of *National Review*, now a senior fellow at the Discovery Institute, and as a fellow congregant some years ago at the Georgetown Synagogue in Washington.

I consulted my friend, debate coach, and super literary lawyer, Bob Barnett, whose representation led me back to Simon & Schuster, which had published two of my previous books, but this time to the religious imprint Howard Books and its very able, spiritual, and enthusiastic publisher, Jonathan Merkh; editor-in-chief, Becky Nesbitt; senior editor, Philis Boultinghouse; and associate editor, Jessica Wong. My executive assistant, Rayanne Bostick, has overseen this work, as she ably and steadfastly does most other parts of my life.

David Klinghoffer and I began our work together in long conversations about my personal religious history, why and how I observe the Sabbath, and how important it was to me to portray the Sabbath in this book in a way that was appealing to readers who are Jewish and those who are not. David is Sabbath observant and a scholarly and eloquent gentleman and writer. He has been a great help in informing, organizing, and assisting me to record my thoughts. He has also been patient in response to my aggressive rewriting and picky editing. This book is, after all, a very personal statement by me about the Sabbath, and I needed to own every word in it.

While every Jew inherits the Jewish tradition as a birthright, our rabbis serve as indispensable guides in understanding its deeper meanings. Rabbi Genack was regularly involved in discussions about the book, as was Rabbi Irving "Yitz" Greenberg, and my two congregational rabbis, Barry Freundel of the Georgetown Synagogue and Daniel Cohen of Congregation Agudath Shalom in Stamford, Connecticut. Rabbi Gil, Student of the Orthodox Union Press, kindly assisted in reviewing the manuscript. I also had very fruitful interactions with Christian clergy and friends about this book. Needless to say, in this, as in every other aspect of my life, my wife, Hadassah, has been my most important partner and muse, and my children and grandchildren have been my inspiration.

APPENDIX:

FURTHER READING AND RESOURCES

I f, as I hope, you feel moved to explore the gift of rest that God offers us all, you may well want to know more about the practices, history and reasons behind the institution of *Shabbat*. With that in mind, I recommend to you two brief and illuminating books: Rabbi Abraham Joshua Heschel's *The Sabbath*, beautifully written and richly evocative, and Rabbi Aryeh Kaplan's *Sabbath: Day of Eternity*, a superb and concise introduction to traditional Sabbath practice. Heschel's is the philosophical approach, Kaplan's the more practical.

For more about the philosophy behind Jewish faith and observance, Heschel's *God in Search of Man* is an important book that has launched many a spiritual quest. In my thinking and writing on the subject I have also drawn repeatedly on the works of Rabbi Joseph B. Soloveitchik. Though he wrote no single book on the Sabbath, his two best-known works are *Lonely Man of Faith* and *Halakhic Man*, which together offer an introduction to his unique philosophical and theological melding of tradition and modernity.

Pope John Paul II wrote an eloquent and moving 1998 apostolic letter, *Dies Domini*, calling for the revival of Sabbath observance. There has, in fact, been a resurgence of interest in the Sabbath among Christians of many denominations, reflected in several excellent books including Lauren Winner's *Mudhouse Sabbath*, Wayne Muller's *Sabbath: Restoring the Sacred Rhythm of Rest*, and Dorothy C. Bass's *Practicing Our Faith*. In his book *God's Politics*, Pastor Jim Wallis predicts that in coming years, "the concept and discipline of the Sabbath will see a great comeback in the lives of overworked and overstressed people." I hope so.

For the prayers of the Sabbath, the Orthodox Union Press has recently published a traditional prayer book, or *Siddur*, collecting some of Rabbi Soloveitchik's thoughts on the liturgy (*The Koren Mesorat HaRav Siddur*). Also invaluable for understanding prayer is the highly accessible and thorough *Siddur* commentary published by Artscroll (*The Complete Artscroll Siddur*). In this book I have also made extensive use of Rabbi Sir Jonathan Sacks's *Siddur* (*The Koren Sacks Siddur*), an exceptionally handsome volume with crisp, insightful commentary from the chief rabbi of Great Britain. The Conservative Jewish movement's prayer book, with excellent notes on the Sabbath, *Siddur Sim Shalom*. The Reform Movement's prayer book *Mishkan Tefilah*, has won praise for recapturing traditional elements of Jewish prayer life in an accessible way. Both have recently been revised.

A central feature of the Sabbath is study of the Holy Scriptures. Over the millennia, drawing on the ancient oral tradition transmitted by our rabbis, Judaism has assembled a vast and deep literature of Torah commentary explicating the often cryptic Scriptural text. Simply reading a Bible translation is no substitute for seeing the Torah opened and unfolded through the insights of the greatest rabbis, going back thousands of years. For an accessible digest of rabbinic thought on the Five Books of Moses, Artscroll's *Chumash: The Stone Edition* is a standard. (The "ch" in *Chumash* is pronounced as in the Scottish "*loch*." The word simply means Pentateuch, or Torah.) For a Torah commentary emphasizing Hasidic or mystical thoughts from the late chief rabbi or "Rebbe" of the Chabad-Lubavitch movement, Menachem Mendel Schneerson, I read *Chumash: The Gutnick Edition*, published by Kol Menachem. The Conservative Jewish Movement has published a Torah with commentary, *Eytz Chayim*, which has been recognized for its scholarship and insights as has the Reform Jewish Movement's, *The Torah: A Modern Commentary*.

For longer essays on the weekly Torah portion or *parsha*, I find several websites of great use. Chabad.org, Aish.com, OU.org, and ChiefRabbi.org all offer new Torah content each week, connecting the themes of the Torah reading to spiritual and practical concerns in our daily lives. Many traditional Sabbath observers enjoy presenting a *devar Torah*, a brief Torah thought or homily, at their Sabbath table. The new essays published on these websites offer inspiration and insight.

Judaism is a way of life, a philosophy, a comprehensive picture of the world and how it works—and how much better it could work. It can also sometimes be intimidating in the sheer complexity and antiquity of our traditional religious sources. Jews and Christians alike may find it useful to acquire a bit of Jewish "literacy" to make their spiritual journey more accessible. For that purpose I recommend Rabbi Joseph Telushkin's excellent *Jewish Literacy: The Most Important Things to Know About the Jewish Religion, Its People and Its History*, along with any of Telushkin's other fine and highly readable works.

For new students of the Sabbath who want to confront the

APPENDIX

actual sources of our tradition at its roots, Artscroll publishes
an English translation and elucidation of the Talmud's tractate on the Sabbath, in four volumes, the *Schottenstein Edition
of the Talmud—Shabbos*. While this is not light reading by any
means, for the Talmud demands to be studied and not merely
read, Artscroll makes the original Hebrew and Aramaic text
as comprehensible as it possibly could be.

Modern digests of Sabbath law in English are of course
also published. A good one is *Shemirath Shabbath: A Guide to
the Practical Observance of Shabbath*, by Rav Yehoshua Y. Neu-
wirth.

For a poignant narrative of one man's spiritual journey of
return to Jewish traditional religious practice, including that
of the Sabbath, dealing also with themes of adoption and personal identity, I commend my collaborator David Klinghoffer's memoir, *The Lord Will Gather Me In*.

As I was working on this book, a gifted Jewish writer,
Judith Shulevitz, published her personal and philosophical
exploration of the day of rest, *The Sabbath World: Glimpses of
a Different Order of Time*. Maybe we are witnessing the beginnings of a Sabbath awakening.

Finally, for Jewish readers who wish to undertake the practice of Shabbat, no book can take the place of a wise and compassionate rabbi, acting as mentor and adviser. For Christian
readers, the same is true of a similarly wise and compassionate
pastor, priest, or minister.